DYNAMICS OF JOB-SEEKING BEHAVIOR

DYNAMICS OF JOB-SEEKING BEHAVIOR

By

NANCY DUNCAN STEVENS, Ph.D.

Director
Career Counseling and Placement
and
Associate Professor
Counseling and Student Development
Hunter College, City University of New York

With a Foreword by

John L. Holland, Ph.D.

Professor Emeritus
The Johns Hopkins University

CHARLES C THOMAS • PUBLISHER
Springfield • Illinois • U.S.A.

Published and Distributed Throughout the World by

CHARLES C THOMAS • PUBLISHER
2600 South First Street
Springfield, Illinois 62717

© *1986 by* CHARLES C THOMAS • PUBLISHER

ISBN 0-398-05175-5

Library of Congress Catalog Card Number: 85-20772

With THOMAS BOOKS *careful attention is given to all details of manufacturing and
design. It is the Publisher's desire to present books that are satisfactory as to their physical
qualities and artistic possibilities and appropriate for their particular use.* THOMAS
BOOKS *will be true to those laws of quality that assure a good name and good will.*

Printed in the United States of America
SC-R-3

Library of Congress Cataloging-in-Publication Data

Stevens, Nancy Duncan
    Dynamics of job-seeking behavior.

    Bibliography: p.
    Includes index.
    1. Job hunting — Psychological aspects. I. Title.
HF5382.7.S74   1985   650.1'4   85-20772
ISBN 0-398-05175-2

To the memory of Anna and Chester Stevens
— two friends who were always there.

FOREWORD

The process of finding a job has rarely been regarded as a problem that is worthy of scientific · investigation. A search of the educational-psychological-sociological literature will turn up only a few sporadic and unconnected studies, and most of these are concerned with either the mechanics of job seeking (resume writing, sources of occupational information) or with the demographics of job winners and losers.

In contrast, Stevens' book is a magnificent, scientific and practical island in the current sea of job-seeking books, techniques and placement services. Her lifetime experience as a placement and counseling practitioner, researcher and thinker has resulted in a book that I expect to become the classic text in placement.

Stevens has provided placement specialists and career counselors with a coherent and comprehensive account of the research on job-seeking behavior that stems largely from her long-term research program. She also provides a studied typology of "positive," "negative" and "transitional" job-seeking behavior that organizes the data for understanding and application.

These diagnostic ideas are then strengthened by a comprehensive chapter on counseling ideas for helping people with placement problems. This eclectic chapter is a rich mine of diverse orientations to the counseling process.

Finally, Stevens reviews the popular theories of career development for their contributions to job-seeking behavior and creates "a holistic process theory of vocational development" from the older theories and her "dynamics of job-seeking behavior." This developmental theory of job seeking provides a bridge between making a vocational choice and its application which will be useful to practitioners, researchers and theorists.

At this time, Stevens' book is the only publication that integrates job-finding research, theory and practice with current career development theory and practice. This task is accomplished in a coherent, imaginative and persuasive manner.

John Holland

PREFACE

This book is about three job-seeking behavior patterns, each reflecting unique personality dynamics as well as levels of vocational development. Job-seeking behavior is the vocational behavior that is the bridge between making an occupational choice and adjusting in a new job to the organization. Consequently, what has emerged is a holistic process theory of vocational development. The middle section of a continuum of vocational development has now fallen in place.

The book is intended for practitioners in the field of job placement who help individuals find jobs, especially for those interviewers and counselors who wonder why a given job seeker does not get a job. Counselor trainers also will find this book useful in training vocational counselors because it focuses on the dynamics of a vocational behavior that are part of the continuum of vocational development and which have been ignored up to this time.

Throughout the book, the terms "placement interviewer" and "placement counselor" are used interchangeably. Either of these may be assigned to staff members who interview clients in a placement service. On the one hand, the term "counselor" implies that the staff member has a degree in counseling. On the other hand, this is not to say that the "interviewer" does not also have a degree in counseling, but it is possible that he or she may not.

Theories of vocational development have focused on the process individuals go through when making an occupational choice. Some theories have extended their focus to cover the process of people adjusting to their first job and establishing themselves in the world of work. These theories bring understanding of the behavior that is exhibited at the two ends of a vocational development continuum. A few of these theories have implied that after people have crystallized and specified a vocational goal, they then obtain a job with which to try out the field of work they have chosen.

As a practicing counselor in the field of job placement, it became evident to me that not all job seekers coming to a placement office in search of information about job opportunities succeeded in obtaining a job that they desired. This was often observed for individuals who seemed to meet all of the employer's requirements for the job, and it aroused my curiosity. Why did some job seekers obtain the jobs that they desired, while others equally well qualified did not? Theories of vocational development did not embrace job-seeking behavior, and so my research studies were undertaken in the setting of the job placement office to determine a better understanding of the personal factors operating in the success, or lack of success, of people in obtaining a job.

I wish to acknowledge those whose influence has brought me to the point where I felt the need to write this book. I doubt that I would have ever started to write professionally if it was not for Professor Emeritus Robert Hoppock of New York University who got me started as his co-author of several articles. I am also indebted to the late Professor Philip J. Zlatchin of New York University and to Professor Emeritus Milton Schwebel of Rutgers, The State University of New Jersey, both of whom encouraged me to examine job-seeking behavior from a theoretical construct. I was also influenced by Professor Emeritus Alva C. Cooper, Hunter College, City University of New York, who encouraged me to conduct my second and third studies on job-seeking behavior patterns, and who also shared her professional library with me when I was writing this book. I am indeed indebted to Professor Emeritus John Holland of The Johns Hopkins University for his recognition of my research and his supportive encouragement to publish.

I am also most appreciative of the assistance of two of my professional colleagues in the field, Barry Lustig, Director of the Professional Development Institute of the Federation Guidance and Employment Service, and Daralee Shulman, career counselor. They were most generous with their time in discussing internal barriers that affect vocational behaviors.

I wish to express my indebtedness to Maria La Russo, Thomas Murphy, Marion Percival and Paula Wicklow of the staff of Career Counseling and Placement, Hunter College, for their willingness to serve as sounding boards for some of the ideas expressed in my manuscript, and to Susan Kriegel Rosenman, former staff counselor, who over a span of time has urged me to write this book and who assisted with the editing. I am also indebted to Lena Carillo and Barbara Hughes for typing the manuscript and to Mary Stern who assisted me in researching the literature, in editing my copy and in handling the overall operation of the manuscript production. Their cooperative efforts are very much appreciated.

Nancy Duncan Stevens

CONTENTS

LIST OF FIGURES

LIST OF TABLES

DYNAMICS OF JOB-SEEKING BEHAVIOR

Chapter One

WORK AND JOB-SEEKING BEHAVIOR

A cultural construct of our society that stems from a Judeo-Christian ethic is that the time of most individuals be spent in work-oriented rather than in pleasure-oriented activities (Stevens, 1966). Consequently, a great many men and women in all stations of life have found work that is either full time, part time or volunteer at some time in their lives.

MEANING OF WORK

For most of us, work is necessary in our industrial and technological society because of the basic requirements for living in affluent as well as in depressed times. No longer do we live in the agricultural society of yesteryear when a family made their living off the land by growing their crops, butchering their meat, bartering their eggs, and building their own shelter and barns for their livestock from the lumber that was cut from the woodlot. Today, work provides us with the monetary means to obtain the basic necessities as well as some of the pleasures of life.

For many individuals, work seems to solve a fundamental need which goes beyond the provision of the basic needs of living. Psychological needs are met by work. Shertzer (1977) identifies at least five such psychological needs.

He states that work can be a means for achieving mastery over situations, people, ideas and machines. For some others, it may be the means of obtaining approval from significant others, be they in the place of work or in the individual's social circle. Work also provides the opportunity to belong to a group of people who are co-workers and to develop friendships which can bring emotional satisfaction and widen one's social horizons.

The need for status or prestige can be met by a person's job. This is especially so if the job is one of responsibility and of marked achievement. For those individuals who have the need to serve others, work can provide that focus. Salespeople, accountants, teachers, counselors and

3

social workers are only some of the workers who have expressed to a placement interviewer the following feeling: "I like my work because I can help people."

Even after retirement, many individuals continue to seek a work activity in order to make their life more meaningful. Such work may be a vocation or it may be an avocation. This is frequently done to earn money to supplement Social Security payments in order to survive economically. However, there can be other reasons, too. There are many retirees who miss the time structure that working establishes. Others feel lost without work when work gives them a sense of identity and a feeling of self-worth. For some, work provides the outlet for a creative expression of the individual's personality.

For others, work provides the opportunity to use a developed skill and to use the expertise one has obtained over the years. It may also lessen the boredom of those whose personality lacks inner resources to fall back on. It can help make the individual feel useful and needed.

Deeper psychological needs may also be met through work. Menninger (1964) identifies an unconscious need as an outlet "for the hostile, aggressive drive which is a major source of psychic energy. Work, even pleasurable, is usually an effort to master the environment. It is carried out 'against' something, or to surmount, solve, or control something.

"The chief motive to work, therefore, may be conceived as an unconscious striving which is consciously adapted to meet the realistic requirements of living." Any or all of these needs may motivate an individual to seek satisfaction in work.

Needless to say, not all people find work to be meaningful. Neff (1977) indicates that there are people who find many negative meanings to work, so that they appear to be alienated from work rather than to be motivated by it. This can range from indifference to work, to a sociopathic aversion to it. Some people can have a maladaptive response to work that may include such personality difficulties as relating to authority figures and interacting with their colleagues. For them, work can raise feelings of anger, fear, inferiority and/or self-depreciation. Work, therefore, does not generate a positive meaning under such circumstances.

Alienation can also be the result of changing labor market conditions, such as when workers whose former jobs have become obsolete are retrained for new technological jobs that need to be filled. Many people can find this change difficult, especially if they do not like the new tasks for which they are being trained. Should their new work fail to fit their self-image, alienation from work can result.

Alienation to work can also be caused by an individual's values which do not place primary importance on earning money, being deeply involved in a job, or in working as its own reward. For them, a job may be considered the means by which the intrinsic things that they do value are made economically possible; that is, whether it is in raising a family, owning a sailing craft, attending the theatre, painting or sculpting, taking courses, traveling or eating in the best restaurants, etc.

However, even for those who are alienated by work, it can be important for them to be engaged in an activity that is meaningful. Work is the means by which their personal goals and avocations can be supported, unless they are fortunate enough to have a private income at their disposal which will underwrite their desired activities. Therefore, most people, regardless of their personal motivations, seek work even in either a booming economic labor market or in a deeply recessed one. The behavior of most individuals, therefore, is job seeking.

HOW PEOPLE FIND JOBS: MYTHS AND EXTERNAL FACTORS

Fate, chance or luck certainly seem to be frequently considered as factors by some people as to why they did or did not get a job. How many times has it been said:

"I was lucky to get this job offer."

OR

"I guess I got the job because I was in the right place at the right time."

OR

"I just happened to meet my new employer at my neighbor's barbecue Saturday afternoon."

OR

"I knew it was time for me to get a break. He offered me the job."

Fate, chance or luck appeared to be operating as far as these new employees are concerned. Is this a myth? Possibly. It does seem to be a truism that when an employer is trying to fill a position and the job seeker who meets the basic requirements of the position appears on the scene (and when the *chemistry* between them also seems to be right), a job offer is often made to that individual. In a sense, being in the right place at the right time can also be luck.

Is it? Can it be luck or chance when this happens? Not likely, if job seekers have been actively networking their friends and acquaintances for contacts to approach in the world of work in quest of a job. The tendered job offers are not the effect of chance or luck when these job applicants are actively engaged in contacting employers by sending resumes, actively pursuing job leads from job placement services, visiting personnel or human relations offices and tapping the *hidden* job market by contacting the heads of departments that especially interest them.

By so doing, they are increasing the probability of getting a job by maximizing all conceivable contacts with employers. Consequently, they are in a favorable position to be considered by employers for jobs when they obtain interviews as a result of these approaches. They have made their own luck, as well as their own chance, for obtaining the jobs they desire.

The power of others is sometimes considered to be an important factor in getting a job. Unsuccessful job applicants sometimes say in frustration:

"The placement office didn't get me a job."

OR

"I have no influential friends who can get me a job."

Is this a myth? In a very real sense, it is. No one can *get* someone else a job: neither a friend nor a placement interviewer. However, both can give the job applicant information about known job vacancies. Both can assist the job seeker in getting an interview appointment with the appropriate person who does the hiring. However, it is up to the job applicant to be well prepared for the interview that gives him or her the opportunity to present qualifications for the job that the employer is trying to fill.

Of the same ilk is the following comment: "Only alumni from the prestigious, big name schools can get a job with that company. They wouldn't touch anyone from my school."

Although it is true that many companies will arrange corporate recruiting visits with many prestigious colleges, it is not true that *all* their employees are alumni from these schools, nor is it true that *all* their top managers are necessarily graduates from such colleges.

This myth is accepted by many job seekers who *creatively* misrepresent their academic credentials on their resumes with the names of Ivy

League colleges and other institutions of prestige as the academic institutions that they attended or from which they received their degrees. Although this false information may get them an interview, they often cannot substantiate their claims during the interview, so that they are eliminated from consideration for the job.

It is interesting to note that when job seekers expect the influence of a friend or the power of the name of an academic institution to "get me a job," they are relying on external factors to obtain employment for them.

The economics of the labor market is an external factor that influences the volume of job opportunities for which people may apply. When business is deeply recessed, the number of positions decreases as business needs to retrench for economic survival, and the volume of unemployed persons increases. It is difficult, if not seemingly impossible, for many individuals to find work under depressed labor market conditions.

Difficulty in finding employment also happens when segments of business and industry are affected by technological changes. A large volume of workers, finding their skills to be outmoded, are affected by the loss of their jobs and frequently have poor prospects of finding other jobs. Unless they are retrained to fill the new jobs that a new technology creates, many of them remain unemployed for long periods of time.

Of course, when the economy is booming, there are many positions available. On occasion, there are more positions available than there are workers to fill them—as happened in the decade of the sixties. However, the experience of many placement counselors and employment interviewers is that there are always some job applicants who seem to be unable to get a job, even when the labor market conditions are very good. Because of their experience and training, these job seekers often would seem to be outstanding candidates for given job vacancies. Yet, in following up these applicants, it is frequently discovered that they did not succeed in getting jobs even after they applied for them.

As a result, placement counselors and employment interviewers try to help these job applicants, with specific focus on improving their interview skills, so that they may be more effective during the employment interviews. Placement counselors also assist job seekers in honing their resumes for a more effective presentation of their academic and work backgrounds, so that their resumes may enhance their chances of getting job interviews. Often, this help may be all that is necessary for many such applicants to be successful in obtaining the job they seek.

The job interviewer also finds that there are many individuals who, despite this special assistance, still do not succeed in obtaining desired jobs. For them, revising resumes and developing interview skills are not the total answer to their problem of continuing unemployment. Because they tend to return to the interviewer for job leads time and time again without obtaining jobs, placement interviewers may often consider them to be *unplaceable*.

Placement counselors also have in their case load job seekers who seem able to readily obtain jobs even in a badly recessed labor market when jobs are difficult to find and competition for them is heavy. These are individuals who can effectively use the special help offered to them in job leads, in resume reconstruction and in streamlining interview skills. The placement interviewer recognizes that these job seekers are easy to place in a job (and so they seem to be).

HOW PEOPLE FIND JOBS: INTERNAL FACTORS

There are also internal factors that account for the contrasts in success in obtaining a job, which were typical of the author's experience early in her career as an interviewer in a college engineering placement office. There were two job applicants, both graduating with a mechanical engineering degree, who were seeking a job in industry. They shall be referred to as Frank and Richard.

Frank was the first appointment that day. He made an attractive appearance. He stated that he wanted something in engineering. His placement registration forms that he had filled out for the interview revealed that he had been a student aide to one of the professors in mechanical engineering and had had a summer job in the engineering department of a large industrial manufacturer. He stated that his professor had procured it for him.

In discussing the job vacancies reported to the placement office, he said, "I'll take anything." He really did not seem to care about the type of industry in which he might work and was vague in his responses when the interviewer attempted to explore his preferences regarding salary level and geographic location.

There were three mechanical engineering job vacancies that were on file with the placement office. One was with a sewing machine company; another with an airplane design company. Both of these were with companies within the New York Metropolitan area. The third job was with an automobile company in Michigan. Frank copied the job information so that he could contact the employers. Upon leaving, he commented, "I certainly hope that you can get me a job."

Richard's appointment followed Frank's. He also was neatly dressed. He stammered when he mentioned that he was seeking an entry-level job in mechanical engineering in a manufacturing company. He had no previous experience, but he learned from his professors the names of companies that had previously hired graduates in mechanical engineering, wherein he mailed his resume to fifty of these companies that were in different geographic locations across the country. Two of these companies had invited him to come to their local offices for an exploratory interview, which he planned to do.

He was interested in exploring the three job vacancies that Frank was going to pursue. The interviewer noticed that he was recording the job information effectively, despite a paralyzed right arm. Three weeks later Richard phoned to report that he had gone on four interviews and had had two job offers. One was with the sewing machine company in New York State and the other was with a heavy machinery manufacturing company near Boston, Massachusetts. He reported that he was accepting the job with the sewing machine company because of its expansion into new technologies, even though the salary with the Boston firm would have been higher.

Shortly thereafter, Frank phoned for more job leads. When asked how he had made out with his applications for the job vacancies that previously had been given to him, he replied that he had not yet contacted the employers but that he planned to do so, together with any new job leads that might be given to him. He had taken no action up to that moment in time. As a result, at least one position for which he was going to try to arrange an interview had already been filled by Richard.

How do people get jobs? Why did not Frank get a desired job? Why did Richard get a mechanical engineering job in spite of the physical handicap which might make aspects of his work difficult to perform? Was the success or failure in obtaining a job due to external factors that were beyond their control—that is, chance, influential friends, prestigious institutions or labor market conditions? Or was it due to some internal personal factor over which each individual had control?

Both Frank and Richard gave evidence of wanting to find a job. Each had been given the same job leads. However, Richard had contacted these employers to obtain interviews, whereas Frank had not started to contact the employers by the time Richard had accepted a job with one of the employers whom both had been told about when they visited the placement services. If a person tends to be passive and does not contact an employer with a vacancy for an appointment, he or she certainly is not going to be offered a job.

Frank gave evidence of passivity and dependence when he stated upon ending the interview, "I certainly hope that you can get me a job." The implication is that he is counting on the efforts of the interviewer rather than on his own efforts to get a job. This is in direct contrast to Richard, whose closing remarks were that he would continue to contact the interviewer for more job leads and that he was sending his resumes to companies that interested him in the hope of getting more interviews. Richard's comments gave evidence of independent and goal-oriented behavior. He was using many approaches to find a job: his use of the placement services, networking contacts and the sending of resumes to appropriate companies.

Frank's and Richard's personality characteristics and apparent life-styles of coping are so sufficiently different that they suggest that these may well be the critical factors in determining the success of one and the failure of the other in getting the job they both desired and for which they were both trained.

It was the author's curiosity concerning the reasons for Frank's failure and Richard's success in obtaining a desired job that prompted her to conduct a study on job-seeking behavior. Her initial prediction had been that Frank would get the job he desired and that Richard would have difficulty in obtaining one. Experienced placement interviewers can, and do, detect cues exhibited in an interview by a job-seeking client which frequently provide the interviewer with a hunch or an impression on how successful the client will be in obtaining his or her expressed job goal. Sometimes these interviewers are right and sometimes they are wrong; in this case I was wrong.

SUMMARY

Many people seek jobs regardless of whether work is meaningful to them or if they are alienated from it. People give different reasons for being successful or unsuccessful in getting a job. These reasons are usually external factors such as chance, labor market conditions, graduation from a prestigious school, etc. How one mobilizes his or her personal resources for coping with the job market is an internal factor. It reflects the individual's personality development and is an important internal factor influencing why some people succeed in obtaining a job and why some do not.

Chapter Two reports on three research studies: the initial study that identified three job-seeking behavior patterns and their effect on success in obtaining jobs in the field of education; the second that replicated the first study on the effect of job-seeking behavior patterns of liberal arts college seniors seeking positions in business, government and social service; and the third that studied the personality characteristics associated with each of the three job-seeking behavior patterns. Because these three studies have been the initial probe into the effect of different styles of job-seeking behavior upon successfully obtaining a desired job, they are described and reported in detail.

Chapter Two

RESEARCH ON JOB-SEEKING BEHAVIOR

T hree research studies were conducted by the author from 1954 to
1969 to explore the dynamics of the behavior of individuals seeking
employment with the assistance of their college placement office. These
studies identified not only three styles or patterns of job-seeking behavior and the effect that each pattern had on the applicants' success in
obtaining a desired job but also the personality characteristics that are
associated with these patterns.

THE FIRST STUDY

The thrust of Stevens's (1960, 1962, 1973) initial study was to test the
ability of college placement interviewers to successfully predict the prob-
able success of their registered clients in obtaining a desired job and to
identify aspects of the job-seekers' personality characteristics that affect
the placement interviewers' assessments of their clients. It has been
noticed that experienced interviewers frequently feel hunches about
which of the job applicants in their case load are ready and able to utilize
job vacancy information effectively and, therefore, are able to identify
which ones will be successful in getting jobs. They also feel that they
know who is not ready for job placement help and/or who is unplaceable,
because in the judgment of the interviewers these clients will not succeed
in gaining employment. Frequently, such clients have been seen regu-
larly by placement counselors over a long span of time. Sometimes the
interviewers' hunches are correct, but they are not always so.

To what personality characteristics of their clients are the interviewers
responding? Upon which characteristics are they consciously or uncon-
sciously basing their judgments? It is important to understand these
factors, because, as Kubis and Hunter (1955) pointed out in the decade of
the fifties, employers do react to their impressions of the job applicant in
much the same manner as do the placement interviewers. Personality
characteristics—an inner factor of the individual—are perhaps more

critical to success in getting a job than are some external factors, such as chance, influential friends, labor market conditions, etc.

Pilot Study

In order to determine that the personality of job seekers was affecting the impressions of placement interviewers and employers, it was first necessary to identify the characteristics that were unique to those whom it seemed to the placement interviewer would be easy to *place* in a job, as well as the personal characteristics of those whom it would be difficult to *place*. A pilot study was conducted for this purpose.

Identification of Personality Characteristics

Twenty-four job seekers from a selected sample of registrants with the New York University Placement Services who were seeking jobs in the field of education were tape-recorded verbatim by two placement interviewers for the pilot study. These tapes were typed, read and sorted by the investigator into the following three categories: (1) applicants who seemed to be ready for job vacancy information concerning specific job goals desired in a specified geographic area or areas (Group A); (2) applicants for whom there seemed to be no conclusive impression that they were or were not ready for job vacancy information concerning specific job goals desired in a specified geographic area or areas (Group B); and (3) applicants who did not seem to be ready for job vacancy information concerning specific job goals desired in a specified geographic area or areas (Group C).

It was then determined that in terms of being ready for job placement, those applicants in Group A were high in placement readiness; those in Group B were moderate in placement readiness; and those in Group C were low in placement readiness. The recorded responses of applicants assigned to Groups A, B and C were analyzed for qualitative differences in order to identify the characteristics of high, moderate and low placement readiness, respectively.

Group A: Characteristics of High Placement Readiness

Group A consisted of six cases of the twenty-four which were identified as being ready for job placement assistance. The job applicants in this group were specific in expressing their desired goals in terms of position, field, level and the geographic location in which they wished to work (see Table I).

For example, one man stated: "I want to teach English on the high school level."

Another client specified: "I want a guidance job near my home in Nassau County."

Still another stated: "In regard to [a] college [level job], this decision I have definitely made! I would want to combine teaching with some clinical work."

These job seekers also gave evidence of activity focused on attempting to obtain their desired job goals. They mentioned job campaigns of their own in which they were engaged. During their appointment with the placement interviewer, they assumed the lead in making direct inquiry about the status of their placement service registration forms and job references on file with the service. They were also cooperative about the suggestions made by the interviewer for updating the data recorded on the forms that the placement office sent to the employers, and they were also willing to obtain additional references from faculty and employers.

For example, one person said: "Yes, I know Professor X is in her office on Monday. I'll ask her for a reference then."

Another stated: "I just wanted to see if that additional reference I got from my supervisor arrived yet. I want to be sure that everything is in order."

Their statements also seemed to indicate that they had an objective awareness of themselves in terms of understanding and translating their strengths, weaknesses and needs for the job market.

One woman stated: "I'm not exactly quitting and I'm not exactly fired. It's a question of tenure. They . . . and I think it would be best to change the age level. . . . It's a question of rapport. I think the high school or college level is what I prefer, but I do know that there are not many college vacancies in my field right now."

Another client, desiring to serve as an educational consultant, analyzed her strengths for competition in the job market for this type of job. "It's not a daydream on my part. I do have experience on that level. For the past three years, I've been giving my service to a national educational organization which is interested in the school movement. I made some contributions . . . and I can get supporting references."

Another reported: "I've been contacting employers on my own to see if they have vacancies for which I might qualify . . . but I thought I'd better check with you also. You may have received some job vacancies that I could go after."

Group C: Characteristics of Low Placement Readiness

Individuals in Group C are the job seekers who it was felt were not ready for job placement and, consequently, were examples of low placement readiness. There were five cases in this group.

Without exception, these individuals were indefinite and vague in expressing their job goals, and they seemed to be confused about what job they desired. Only two of the five had been able to indicate a desired field in tentative terms, even though they have been indefinite about the level of job and geographic locale that they desired (see Table I).

For example, one stated: "I think I'd be interested in doing something in the psychology field, that is, if my background can be related to it at all. I don't know if it can.... I guess anything where I can work with children."

Others wanted a job without specifying what job they wanted or desired.

For example, a man demanded: "You get me a job." A woman declared to the interviewer: "Professor A said I should take a job where I can come in and say hello to my folks. Anything will do...." The type of work was unexpressed, even after the interviewer attempted to explore for indications of possible work preferred.

A man stated: "Tell me what job I should take and I'll take it."

Not only were they vague, but sometimes they indicated their confusion by stating that they were uncertain about what job and on which institutional level they should apply.

For example, one person expressed her confusion by saying: "that is the whole trouble. I don't know what I want to teach. If there was anything reasonable and fairly to my liking, I'd have a hard time distinguishing if I wanted it."

The above statements are illustrative of the vague, passive, dependent and floundering qualities that they reveal, and there were other indications of these qualities during their interviews. No mention had been made by these job seekers of job campaigns in which they would be contacting employers about possible available job opportunities. Some of these individuals did not know what an interviewer meant when asked whether they considered sending out their resumes on a job campaign. They also did not inquire into the status of their registration forms and

TABLE I

COMPARATIVE "PROFILES" OF PLACEMENT READINESS FOR
HIGH, MODERATE AND LOW PLACEMENT READINESS IN PILOT STUDY

Placement Readiness		High						Moderate													Low				
		Group A						Group B													Group C				
Categories	Characteristics	1	10	11	14	19	20	2	3	4	5	7	8	9	12	16	18	21	22	23	6	13	15	17	24
Definite	Specific – Position	x	x	x	x	x	x	x			x	x	x	x	x	x							x		
	Specific – Field		x				x	x			x	x	x	x	x	x				x	x			x		
	Specific – Level			x	x	x	x			x	x	x	x	x	x	x										
	Specific – Locale	x		x	x	x	x	x		x	x	x			x	x	x		x	x						
Active	Action–Job Campaign	x	x							x	x	x						x						x	x	
	Cooperation–Forms and References	x		x	x	x	x	x			x	x			x			x	x	x						
Objective	Understanding – Job Choice			x			x																	x		
	Reactions to Job Hunt			x																						
Indefinite	Vague – Position							x				x	x	x	x	x		x		x	x	x	x	x	x	x
	Vague – Level							x	x				x	x	x					x	x	x	x	x	x	x
	Vague – Locale								x													x			x	x
Passive	Hesitancy – Job Campaign, Forms and References									x								x					x	x		
	Expression of Confusion over Locale							x				x	x	x								x	x	x	x	
	Expression of Authority											x	x	x	x											
Subjective	Expression of Fear and Anxiety							x			x		x				x					x	x	x	x	
	Subjective Reactions to Job												x				x						x		x	
	Seductive Responses													x										x	x	

From Nancy D. Stevens, The Relationship of Placement Readiness to Placement Success. Unpublished Dissertation. New York University, 1960.

references as had the individuals in Group A. Actually, they expressed reluctance to obtain current references from faculty and to update the information on their registration forms when they were advised to do so by the interviewer.

One job seeker stated: "I don't know if Professor C will be in his office. I may not be able to get a reference from him."

Another said: "I don't know how to reach Doctor P for a reference. Could you?"

Individuals in this group also gave evidence of feelings and reactions that might be termed unrealistic and which also gave evidence of instability.

One woman reported: "I just love teaching so. I don't know why I love the kids. . . . When I'm with the kids, I feel they are my own. They're so adorable."

Another job seeker, in discussing a specific job lead for which he had the qualifications and met all the job requirements, said: "I'm afraid . . . afraid." He did not apply.

Two clients made statements that seemed to be seductive in a sense. Both of these clients made an effort to engage the interviewer's personal involvement in their seeking a job through flattery.

For example, one job seeker stated: "Uh, . . . I really do think this placement office does a wonderful job . . . the best actually. . . ."

Another stated: "You've been so helpful . . . no wonder everyone loves you so much."

Such statements suggest the possibility that these job seekers may be trying to develop a dependent relationship with a person in authority. They tend to regard the interviewer as having the potential power that will affect their chances of getting a job by either withholding job vacancy notices from them or by making job vacancies available to them.

Group B: Characteristics of Moderate Placement Readiness

Group B consisted of thirteen job seekers who could neither be identified as being easy to place, nor being hard to place. The impression that was given from their responses was that they were exhibiting a mixture of the expressed characteristics of the job seekers in Groups A (high placement readiness) and C (low placement readiness). Therefore, the individuals in Group B were identified as having moderate placement readiness.

Of the thirteen interviewees, one, who had originally been judged as having moderate placement readiness by the investigator in the initial

sorting of the recorded interviews, was later found to have the characteristics of high placement readiness when the person's responses were
analyzed. The interview had been very short in length and that had
contributed to the difficulty in determining initially whether or not the
job seeker would be or would not be easy to place. Due to the first
general impression it gave to the author, it had been assigned to Group B.

It was found that the characteristic responses of twelve of the thirteen
interviewees in the group were actually a mixture of the characteristic
responses of high and low placement readiness. These individuals seemed
to be crystallized as well as confused when discussing their job goals (see
Table I).

For example, one person stated: "I'm interested in work and I would
prefer something in New York City, as I plan to continue my studying
here for my Ph.D." Later in the interview he stated: "I am originally
from Ohio, and I think I would be interested in something in that state. I
would prefer something near my home."

In neither statement did he specifically define his job goal in precise
terms but referred to it as "work" and "something." His two statements
concerning a geographic location were contradictory.

Another man stated specifically that he was interested "in any position
for an English teacher on the Island." When he was asked to identify the
area or areas on Long Island in which he wished to work so that specific
job leads meeting his interest could be identified and reviewed with him,
he replied somewhat vaguely: "I'm not sure."

In some instances these job seekers gave indication that they had
definite goals, but they also gave evidence that occasionally their decisions had been made for them.

One person reported: "It was a last minute decision. . . . It took a good
deal of the summer to decide to leave my job and try for the college
level. Two or three times the suggestion has been made that I try to teach
on the college level, and that suggestion came directly from the New
York State Employment Service, and so I'll try to do it."

Another said: "I've been uncertain about what I wanted to do until
Professor C, who knows me so well, told me she thinks I should be a high
school guidance counselor. What vacancies do you know about?"

In another interview a woman exhibited responses that were a mixture
of the responses of both high and low placement readiness. She had a
specific job goal which had been thought through realistically, but she
showed dependence, if not passivity, by asking the interviewer to contact

employers for her. "I no longer want to teach, but I could use my teaching experience in English with a publishing company." This was a new, specific goal for her. However, toward the end she asked: "There's just one thing. Would you contact the employers for me to see if they could use me?"

A unique characteristic of the individuals in Group B that was observed by inspection of their recorded responses was that they asked more questions than those in the other two groups. Twenty-seven percent of their total responses were in the form of questions as compared to 21 percent for individuals in Group A and 12 percent for those in Group C.

This suggests that the job seekers in Group A undoubtedly did not need to ask as many questions because they had already established their job goals, and that those in Group C did not ask as many questions as individuals in the other two groups because of their passivity. Job seekers in Group B were actively seeking information about job descriptions and salaries for many different fields. They were actively exploring.

Reliability of Placement Readiness Identifications

It was necessary to ascertain the reliability of the placement readiness ratings that were made of the recorded interviews by three experienced placement interviewers. The data collected on the placement readiness evaluations was treated by means of three tests: (1) a test-retest of the evaluations of placement readiness ratings initially made by the investigator on all twenty-four recorded interviews; (2) a test of inter-rater agreement of placement readiness ratings on twelve randomly selected interviews from the total twenty-four interviews; and (3) a test for the reliability of the percentage of agreement on the twelve interviews made by three raters.

Test-Retest Evaluation. The Pearson Product Moment Coefficient of Correlation was used for a test-retest evaluation of the investigator's initial twenty-four placement readiness ratings with the second ratings of the investigator and two other experienced placement interviewers that were made two years later. A minimum of $r = 0.80$ had to be obtained for these ratings to be considered reliable.

An $r = 0.87$ was obtained, showing a high correlation between the initial placement readiness ratings and the later ratings. The ratings were reliable.

Inter-Rater Agreement of Ratings. The evaluations of the placement readiness ratings for twelve of the interviews that were made by three experienced placement interviewers were compared for the amount of agreement in rating among the raters. It was determined that there would have to be an agreement between at least two of the three raters for each interview in order for the ratings of placement readiness to be considered reliable.

Of the thirty-six total ratings, there were twenty-nine ratings where the raters were in total agreement, and there were only seven ratings where there was disagreement. Of this seven, the rater agreement was two out of three. The rater disagreement was only one step off out of a possible total of three steps.

The ratings of the three judges were found to be reliable.

Percentage of Agreement of Ratings. Using the statistical formula for the reliability of the percentage of agreement, it was found that 81 percent of the total ratings were in agreement, with a *true* percentage of agreement on placement readiness ratings between 68.18 percent and 93.82 percent. Nineteen percent of the ratings were in disagreement.

The ratings were found to be reliable.

Developmental Process

Evidence from the analysis of the interview responses for Groups A, B and C suggested that there was a developmental process in operation. Table I indicates that all responses for Group A were crystallized and specific, action oriented and objective, whereas those for Group C were indefinite, vague, passive and subjective. Responses from Group B were scattered between the types of responses made by Groups A and C. In addition, it has been noted that more questions were asked by Group B than by the other two groups, which suggested that individuals in this group were exploring.

Three of the interviews turned out to be with one person and were taped over a period of fourteen weeks. The first interview was assigned to Group C and was assessed as low in placement readiness. The second interview six weeks later was assigned to Group B and was identified as having characteristics that were typical of the individuals in both Groups A and C. Consequently, the responses were typical of moderate placement readiness. The third interview had been recorded fourteen weeks after the first one. It was also assigned to Group B. However, in analyzing the responses, it was observed that many more responses were typical of those in Group A than had been expressed in the second interview.

Consequently, there were fewer responses that were characteristic of Group C, and this suggested that there had been developmental movement toward a greater specification of job goals.

Analysis of the Group B interviews also indicated that this was a group of job seekers who had begun the process of obtaining information about jobs and fields of work. They were beginning to explore and assess their vocational options.

The observed characteristics of the behaviors identified by the analysis of the interview responses made by job seekers in Groups A, B and C suggested the behaviors that Ginzberg et al. (1951) identified in three periods of vocational development. The relationship between job-seeking behavior patterns and theories of vocational development will be explored in detail in Chapter Six.

Summary of the Pilot Study

1. Three patterns or styles of job-seeking behavior were identified, each with characteristically different behavior.

2. Each pattern could be described in terms of a placement readiness level: high, moderate and low. Job seekers with high placement readiness (Group A) were identified as being easy to place, because they expressed specific job goals and exhibited independent and self-actualized behavior.

Individuals with low placement readiness (Group C) were identified as being difficult to place in a job. This was because they were indefinite and vague about their job goals, and were passive and dependent to the point of permitting (and sometimes seeking out) others to make vocational decisions for them.

Those for whom it was difficult to assess if they would be easy to place or would be difficult to place (Group B) exhibited in their responses a mixture of the characteristics found in both the high and low placement readiness levels. They were considered to have moderate placement readiness. They were definite in some responses concerning their job goals and vague in other responses about them. Compared to the other two levels, individuals in Group B tended to seek the most information about their job options.

3. The movement from vagueness and dependence identified in low placement readiness toward crystallization and independence identified in high placement readiness reflects a developmental process.

The Development of the Placement Readiness and Placement Success Scales

Although the different characteristic behaviors that are exhibited in seeking work were successfully identified by experienced interviewers, it was important to test the effect of each job-seeking behavior pattern upon the individual's success in obtaining a desired job. It was also of interest to establish whether the interviewer's prediction of the job seeker's success in obtaining a job would be more accurate if that prediction was based on an objective analysis of the individual's interview behaviors, rather than on an overall impression of the client.

Therefore, it was necessary to measure the placement readiness of job seekers on a new population, as well as to measure their level of success in obtaining the jobs they desired. Three Placement Readiness Scales and a Placement Success Scale were designed and are described as follows:

Placement Readiness Scale

The Placement Readiness Scale was designed for an analysis of interview responses in topic areas that can arise in a typical job placement interview (see Fig. 1).

The Placement Readiness Scale is a ten-dimension, five-point scale. The established characteristics of placement readiness as identified in the pilot study became a primary source upon which the construction of the scale was based. Because each of the interview behaviors of the job seekers in Groups A, B and C was uniquely different and because they also fitted the distinct periods of vocational development as described by Ginzberg (1951), his developmental periods of Specification, Crystallization and Exploration were used to denote the three highest dimensions on the Placement Readiness Scale. Therefore, *Specification* was used for point 5, the highest point, and denoted job seekers who were able to express a specific goal. *Crystallization* was used for point 4 and denoted job seekers who were able to crystallize their field of interest and their job goal. *Exploration* was used for point 3 and denoted those clients who were exploring possible fields of interest and who seemed to evaluate their fields of choice after receiving job information.

Ginzberg also described the different behaviors of individuals attempting to make an occupational choice. He found that some people were passive and sometimes could be described as floundering. This parallels the characteristics of the job seekers in Group C. Therefore, the term *Confusion* was used for point 2. It denoted those job seekers who, in trying to express their job goals, seemed to be confused and appeared to remain so, even after job information had been presented to them. The term *Passivity* was used for point 1, the lowest point of the scale, and denoted those clients who indicated no action on their own behalf, either in seeking jobs or in choosing their job goals.

	5 Specification	4 Crystallization	3 Exploration	2 Confusion	1 Passivity
I Job Desired					
II Field Desired					
III Level Desired					
IV Job Requirements					
V Geographic Locale					
VI Job Application					
VII Job Campaign					
VIII Salary					
IX Registration Forms					
X Reference Forms					

Figure 1. Placement Readiness Scale. From Nancy D. Stevens, *The Relationship of Placement Readiness to Placement Success.* Unpublished Dissertation. New York University, 1960.

Ten topic areas were identified from the taped interviews of the pilot study that were possible to be covered in any interview for job placement. These topic areas formed the ten dimensions of the scale and were as follows: (I) Job Desired, (II) Field of Interest, (III) Level of Job, (IV) Job Requirements, (V) Geographic Location, (VI) Job Application, (VII) Job Campaign, (VIII) Salary, (IX) Registration Forms, and (X) Reference Forms. Not every topic area needed to be covered in any one interview.

Definitions identifying the behaviors to be found in each of the ten topic areas for each of the five dimensions are listed in the Appendices.

Scoring. To obtain a quantitative measure of placement readiness, the interviewers' ratings of the job seekers' response characteristics were made immediately following the interview and were recorded by a check mark in the different topic areas that were discussed during the interview under the appropriate scale dimension of: (1) Passivity, (2) Confusion, (3) Exploration, (4) Crystallization, (5) Specification. Each rating was given a weighted score which corresponded to the number of the dimension in which it fell. For example, if a client was judged to be specific (Dimension 5) in expressing the desired salary of the job that he or she was seeking (Topic Area VIII), the rating was given the value of five points.

The numerical values given to the ratings that fell into any of the five columns of the scale for any of the topic areas were totalled for each column separately. The sums of all five columns were added and then divided by the number of topic areas for which the interview responses and questions had been rated. The averages obtained were carried to two decimal places for a placement readiness score.

Placement Readiness Scores. The following are the placement readiness scores that determined the level of placement readiness:

Score Points	Placement Readiness Levels
1–1.99	Very Low Placement Readiness
2–2.99	Low Placement Readiness
3–3.99	Moderate Placement Readiness
4–4.99	High Placement Readiness
5	Very High Placement Readiness

Overall Impression Readiness Rating Scale

In the pilot study, one interview had given the impression of belonging to Group B: that is, it was an example of moderate placement readiness. However, an analysis of the responses revealed that it should have been placed in Group A, in that responses were characteristic of high placement readiness. Therefore, it was necessary to develop and test an overall impression readiness rating in order to evaluate the interviewer's immediate impression of the job seeker's success in getting a job.

The Overall Impression Readiness Rating Scale is a one-dimension, five-point scale consisting of the following points: (1) Very Low Placement Readiness, (2) Low Placement Readiness, (3) Moderate Placement Readiness, (4) High Placement Readiness, and (5) Very High Placement Readiness (see Fig. 2).

(5) Very High	(4) High	(3) Moderate	(2) Low	(1) Very Low

Figure 2. Overall Impression Readiness Rating Scale. From Nancy D. Stevens, *The Relationship of Placement Readiness to Placement Success.* Unpublished Dissertation. New York University, 1960.

Scoring. The interviewer's rating of his or her impression of the job seeker's placement readiness was made immediately following the interview by checking the appropriate box. Arbitrary weights were assigned and were equivalent to the number of the scale point. For example, if the interviewer felt that his or her overall impression of the job-seeking interviewee was low in placement readiness (the second point on the scale), the rating score was also two.

Placement Prediction Rating Scale

The Placement Prediction Rating Scale was constructed to measure the accuracy of the interviewer's prediction of the job seeker's success in obtaining a desired job by comparing this prediction of success with the actual success in getting the job. This prediction was based not only on the interviewer's awareness of the individual's level of placement readiness but also on his or her knowledge of possible opportunities in the job seeker's field of interest.

The Placement Prediction Rating Scale is a five-point scale consisting of the following categories: (1) Unplaceable, (2) Hard to Place, (3) Potentially Placeable, (4) Placeable, (5) Easy to Place. It is a one-dimension scale (see Fig. 3).

The term *unplaceable* indicated that the interviewer had no expectation of being able to *place* the job seeker in a desired job. This was due to the apparent inability of the individual to crystallize a job goal and to mobilize personal resources for the purpose of integrating skills, experiences, training and other reality factors which are so necessary for obtaining job goals. The individual gave no evidence of having made any effort to seek a job. *Hard to Place* indicated that the interviewer felt that it would be difficult to place the job seeker because of exhibited vague goals and dependent behavior. *Potentially Placeable* indicated that the interviewer expected to be able to *place* the job seeker upon completion of requirements for the desired job or which were currently in the

(5) Easy to Place	(4) Placeable	(3) Potentially Placeable	(2) Hard to Place	(1) Unplaceable

Figure 3. Placement Prediction Rating Scale. From Nancy D. Stevens, *The Relationship of Placement Readiness to Placement Success.* Unpublished Dissertation. New York University, 1960.

process of being met. The term *Placeable* indicated that the interviewer expected to be able to place the job seeker in a desired job because the individual would meet the job requirements and there were job opportunities available in his or her field. *Easy to Place* indicated that the interviewer expected to have no difficulty in placing the job seeker in a desired job, because the individual had realistic and specific job goals, self-actualized behavior, and met the requirements for jobs in his or her chosen field.

Scoring. The interviewer's placement prediction rating of the job seeker was made immediately following the completion of the job placement interview by checking the appropriate rating that designated his or her prediction. Arbitrary weights were assigned to each rating that were equivalent to the number of the point on the scale. Therefore, if the interviewer's prediction for a given interviewee was that he or she was *Placeable* (the fourth point on the scale), the score was also four.

Placement Success Scale

The Placement Success Scale was constructed to measure the job seeker's level of success in obtaining a job that he or she desired. The placement success ratings were necessary for identifying the most successful job-seeking behavior pattern, as identified by the characteristics of high, moderate and low placement readiness, and evaluated by the Placement Readiness Scale and the Overall Impression Readiness Rating Scale. It was also used to test the accuracy of the interviewer's prediction ratings of placement success. These four scales formed the basis upon which the relationship of the characteristics of high, moderate and low placement readiness to success in obtaining a job was ascertained.

Seven criteria were selected as categories for measuring job placement success and they formed the following categories: (1) whether a job was or was not obtained; (2) in the desired work setting—that is, in the setting of education or some other setting; (3) on the desired level, or the level of second or third choice, or of an unpreferred level; (4) in the desired geographic locale, or in a locale of second or third choice, or in an unpreferred locale; (5) at the desired salary or better, minimum salary, or below the minimum salary; (6) in the desired field, or in a field of second or third choice, or in an unpreferred level; and (7) within a period of time consisting of one, two or three months or more of the initial interview (see Fig. 4).

Name_____

I.   1. Client obtained job.

     2. Client did not obtain job.

II. 3. Client obtained job in setting of Education.

     4. Client obtained job in setting of Business & Industry.

If client obtained job in desired setting:

III. Level

     A. Obtained job in desired level
     B. Obtained job on level of second or third choice
     C. Obtained job on undesired level

IV. Geographic Location
     A. Obtained job in desired locale
     B. Obtained job in locale of second or third choice
     C. Obtained job in unpreferred locale

V. Salary
     A. Obtained desired salary, or better
     B. Obtained minimum salary
     C. Obtained salary below minimum level that could be considered

VI. Field
     A. Obtained job in desired field
     B. Obtained job in field of second or third choice
     C. Obtained job in unpreferred field

VII. Time
     A. Obtained job within 1 month of initial interview
     B. Obtained job within 2 months of initial interview
     C. Obtained job within 3 months, or more, of initial interview

Figure 4. Placement Success Scale. From Nancy D. Stevens, *The Relationship of Placement Readiness to Placement Success*. Unpublished Dissertation. New York University, 1960.

Scoring. The Placement Success Scale was scored as follows:

Categories	Points
I. Client Obtained a Job	1
Client Did Not Obtain a Job	0
II. Client Obtained Job in Education* (if this was goal)	2
Client Obtained Job in Business*	1
Client Obtained Job in Government*	1
III. Client Obtained Job at Desired Level	3
Client Obtained Job at Level of Second or Third Choice	2
Client Obtained Job at Unpreferred Level	1
IV. Client Obtained Job in Desired Geographic Location	3
Client Obtained Job in Location of Second or Third Choice	2
Client Obtained Job in Unpreferred Location	1
V. Client Obtained Desired Salary or Better	3
Client Obtained Minimum Salary Desired	2
Client Obtained Salary Below Minimum Level That Can Be Considered	1
VI. Client Obtained Job in Desired Field	3
Client Obtained Job in Field of Second or Third Choice	2
Client Obtained Job in Unpreferred Field	1
VII. Client Obtained Job Within One Month of Initial Interview	3
Client Obtained Job Within Two Months of Initial Interview	2
Client Obtained Job Within Three Months of Initial Interview	1

Placement Success Scores. The scores of each category were added and the sum was divided by the number of scored sections. There could be a

---

*If the client's desired job goal is in the Business setting and the job obtained is in Business, then the score is two. However, if the job goal is in Business and a job is obtained in either Education or in Government, then the score is one because it is not in the desired setting. The same holds true should the desired job goal be the Education or the Government setting.

maximum of seven categories scored. Depending on the amount of information reported and recorded on the job that the individual obtained, it could be less than seven.

The averaging of the category scores resulted in the following fixed scores for those who obtained jobs in their desired setting:

Raw Scores	Placement Success Scores
18	2.57
17	2.43
16	2.29
15	2.14
14	2.00
13	1.88
12	1.71
11	1.57

For those who obtained a job outside of their desired setting, their placement success score was 1. Those who did not obtain a job at all received a score of 0.

The following levels were assigned to the placement success scores:

Scores	Success Levels
2.43–2.57	High Placement Success
2.00–2.29	Moderate Placement Success
0.00–1.86	Low Placement Success

The rationale behind this assignment of values to levels of placement success was as follows: a score of 0 indicated no success at all in obtaining a job; a score of 1 indicated success in obtaining a job outside the setting of first choice. For example, if the goal was a job in Education but the job obtained was in Business instead of Education, then the position obtained was not in the preferred setting. Therefore, it was not considered as much of a placement success as if it had been obtained in the field of Education.

Those who did accept a job in a desired setting, but with a success score of 1.57, 1.71, or 1.86, were low in placement success compared to the obtained scores of 2.43 and 2.57 that were the two highest scores in the range and were clearly the scores for high placement success. The scores 2.00, 2.14, and 2.29 were in the middle range and were considered to represent moderate placement readiness.

The Design of the First Study

Three styles of job-seeking behavior, each identified as a placement readiness level with different personality characteristics, were identified in the pilot study after assessment of interview responses by experienced interviewers. To test the validity of their evaluations of the job seekers' level of readiness for job placement, it was necessary for the interviewers to evaluate a new population of job seekers in terms of their placement readiness and success in obtaining a job. This initial study is presented in detail.

Population

The setting for this study was the New York University Placement Services, which was a centralized placement service that assisted the university's students and alumni who were seeking full-time and part-time positions.

The population was drawn from a random sampling of one hundred job seekers having an initial interview with any one of four interviewers in the education division of the placement services. They were seeking full-time jobs in teaching, supervision and administration in the fields of administration, art, audiovisual education, core education, elementary education, mathematics, music, nursing education, women's physical education, psychological and guidance services, reading, science education, special education and speech education at the elementary, secondary, college and agency levels.

These were fields for which there was sufficient opportunity in the labor market to find jobs, because job vacancies for professionals were being reported to the placement services by employers who wished to hire replacements. The factor of lack of opportunity in the market was controlled by this method of field selection so that the research hypothesis would have a fair test.

Another criterion in selecting the sample population was that the job seekers appear to be of the white race. This criterion was introduced solely to avoid a possible prejudicial factor that could affect the test of the hypothesis. The fact that this method of identification was not reliable did not affect the study, because it was necessary only to exclude those clients who might have evoked prejudicial attitudes from the employer, even though the New York State Fair Employment Practices Law was in operation. It was always possible not to hire someone for reasons of prejudice and to mask the fact by giving a more acceptable reason, such as lack of a certain type of experience or a course in training, etc., on the part of the job applicant.

Collection of the Data

Four experienced placement interviewers evaluated randomly selected job seekers, immediately following their interviews with them, by using the Placement Readiness Scale, the Overall Impression Readiness Rating Scale and the Placement Prediction Rating Scale to obtain measures of placement readiness levels and interviewer predictions of success in getting a job for the individuals in the sample.

Expressed Job-Seeker Goals. A follow-up was conducted ten months later to learn about details of the jobs that these job seekers had accepted. This was considered to have been a sufficient length of time for these individuals to have procured a job, if they were able to do so. The job information was compared to their initial statements of the job they desired and was rated accordingly on the Placement Success Scale.

Reliability of Expressed Job-Seeker Goals. Because it was possible that these clients might alter their initially stated job goals, it was necessary to establish the reliability of the job seekers' expressed goals.

Therefore, one-fourth (twenty-five) of the population under study was randomly selected from the interview schedule to be contacted by the investigator about their job goals. This was done three weeks after their initial interviews with their placement interviewers.

This information was recorded and any changes from the initially stated goals were noted. For example, another item might have been added to the original statement of preferred geographic locale in which the interviewees wished to work, or a lower or higher salary preference might have been stated, etc.

A percentage of the number of cases in agreement was set arbitrarily at 80 percent for there to be considered a reliable consistency of goals expressed by these clients.

It was found that twenty-one job seekers, or 84 percent of the subsample, expressed the same goals the second time that they were asked about them as they did in their first interview. The individuals in this subsample were consistent in their responses. Therefore, the consistency of responses about job goals that were initially expressed in the first placement interview was considered to be reliable for the population.

Methodology

Because of the highly experimental nature of the research, the Chi-Square Test was used to make three qualitative analyses of the data that was obtained from the Placement Success Scale, the Overall Impression Readiness Rating Scale and the Placement Prediction Rating Scale. The data about the jobs that these job seekers obtained was collected from a follow-up study made ten months after the first interview at the placement services. This job data was evaluated by the Placement Success Scale in order to determine the level of placement success that each job seeker obtained.

These observed results were then compared to the expected results of the null hypothesis and were tested by the Chi-Square formula:

$$x^2 = \left[\frac{(fo-fe)^2}{fe} \right]$$

For such an evaluation, it was necessary to test the null hypothesis: the probability of placement success is the same for all individuals regardless of their level of placement readiness. The null hypothesis was tested at the 0.05 level of significance at $(n-1)$, or two degrees of freedom.

The Chi-Square Test was also used to test the effectiveness of the interviewer's overall impression of the job seeker and his or her prediction of client success in getting a job with the job seeker's actual success in obtaining a desired job goal.

The Findings

It was established that there is a highly significant relationship between the characteristics of high placement readiness and high placement success, between the characteristics of low placement readiness and low placement success, and between the characteristics of moderate placement readiness and moderate placement success (see Table II).

It was established that job seekers with crystallized, specific job goals and independent, self-actualized behavior were the most effective in

TABLE II

RELATIONSHIP OF PLACEMENT READINESS TO PLACEMENT SUCCESS FOR
MEN AND WOMEN IN EDUCATION

Placement Readiness	Placement Success			
	H	M	L	x^2
High	28	4	0	42.879 *p $<$ .001
Moderate	12	17	0	15.739 *p $<$ .001
Low	9	4	16	7.487 *p $<$ .05

*The tabled x^2 at 2df and at the .05 level of confidence is 5.991. Since the results are greater than the tabled x^2, the results are highly significant.

The obtained x^2 for high and moderate placement readiness and high and moderate placement success is even higher than the tabled x^2= 13.815 at the .001 level of confidence.

From Nancy D. Stevens, The Relationship of Placement Readiness to Placement Success. Unpublished Dissertation. New York University, 1960.

obtaining a job that they desired, and that those with vague, confused job goals and dependent, passive behavior were the most ineffective in their efforts to obtain a desired job.

The interviewers' overall impression of the job seekers' readiness for placement was successful only in identifying those job seekers with the characteristics of high placement readiness who obtained high placement success. Their overall impressions of job seekers with moderate and low placement readiness were unsuccessful (see Table III).

Successful predictions of placement success levels were made for job seekers who had actually obtained high and low placement success. The behaviors exhibited by these job seekers were clear-cut in their extremes, and, so, it was not surprising that the predictions for these two groups were significant (see Table IV). However, the characteristic behaviors of individuals with moderate placement success were not clear-cut because of the typical mixture of specificity and vagueness and dependence and independence exhibited in the interview behaviors. The Chi-Square Test result was not significant for this group.

TABLE III

RELATIONSHIP OF OVERALL IMPRESSIONS OF HIGH, MODERATE AND LOW
PLACEMENT READINESS TO PLACEMENT SUCCESS

Placement Readiness	Placement Success			
	H	M	L	x^2
High	25	3	2	33.800 *p .001
Moderate	10	16	5	5.968 NS
Low	7	11	11	1.099 NS

*The tabled x^2 at 2df at the .05 level of confidence is 5.991. Since the obtained x^2 is greater than the tabled x^2, the results are highly significant for the relationship of high placement readiness and placement success. The obtained x^2 is even higher than the tabled x^2 = 13.815 at .001 level of significance. The results are insignificant for moderate and low placement success at the .05 level of significance.

From Nancy D. Stevens, The Relationship of Placement Readiness to Placement Success. Unpublished Dissertation. New York University, 1960.

TABLE IV

RELATIONSHIP OF PREDICTION OF PLACEMENT SUCCESS TO ACTUAL
PLACEMENT SUCCESS

Actual Placement Success	Predictions of Placement Success			
	High	Moderate	Low	x^2
High	22	7	1	23.400 *p $<$ .001
Moderate	6	11	14	3.172 NS
Low	1	11	17	13.470 *p $<$ .01

*The tabled x^2 at 2df at the .05 level of confidence is 5.991. Since the obtained x^2 is greater than the tabled x^2, the results are highly significant for the predicted relationship of high and low placement success. The obtained x^2 for prediction of high placement success is higher than the tabled x^2 at the .001 level of confidence. The obtained x^2 for prediction of low placement success is higher than the tabled x^2 at the .01 level of confidence.

From Nancy D. Stevens, The Relationship of Placement Readiness to Placement Success. Unpublished Dissertation. New York University, 1960.

Difference in Quality of the Scales in Predicting Placement Success

Inasmuch as the null hypotheses concerning the high overall impression of placement readiness and the prediction of high and low placement success were both rejected, it was desirable to test the difference of all the scales in their capability to successfully identify the job seeker's placement success. This was especially needed, in that the Placement Readiness Scale rejected the null hypotheses in each of the three tests concerning the level of placement readiness and its relationship to placement success.

The formula for the Standard Error of the Differences Between Uncorrelated Percentages was used,

$$\sigma SE_{D\%} = \sqrt{PQ\left[\frac{1}{N_1} + \frac{1}{N_2}\right]}$$

where P equals the percentage of times an event occurs, and Q equals the percentage of times an event does not occur, and N equals the number of cases.

There was no significant difference in the quality of one scale over another in predicting an individual's success in obtaining a desired job. However, the results of each of these independent scales indicated that the characteristics of the individual's job-seeking behavior could be identified effectively when his or her placement readiness was rated for characteristic pattern by an objective analysis of the interview content. That is, when the Placement Readiness Scale was used, it was more effective in predicting placement success than was the counselor's own clinically intuitive judgment which was based on an overall impression of the interviewee. The Placement Readiness Scale was effective with each of the three levels of placement readiness.

THE SECOND STUDY

The initial study (Stevens, 1960, 1972) had established the relationship of placement readiness characteristics to success in getting a job for individuals seeking jobs in the profession of education. The second study (1965) focused on liberal arts seniors seeking positions in the fields of business and government. This is a group of job seekers who are more difficult to place compared to job applicants with special training.

The Design of the Study

The purpose of this study was to retest the relationship of high, moderate and low placement readiness to the level of success in getting a job for a population of liberal arts graduating seniors. Job seekers without specific professional and technical degrees might have been expected to have more difficulty finding jobs than those job seekers with a professional degree, such as a degree in business or education. Therefore, graduating seniors expecting to receive the bachelor of arts degree from liberal arts colleges were chosen as a hard test of the hypothesis.

The first study had excluded the possible prejudice of employers from interfering with the test of its hypotheses by selecting only those job seekers who appeared to have been of the white race. However, a reality of the labor market presents the possibility that prejudice might be a factor that can affect the chances of job applicants who may be representative of different races, religions, as well as public versus privately funded colleges.

Population

The population was randomly drawn from the job placement interview schedules at Iona College in New Rochelle, New York, a private church-affiliated men's college, The College of New Rochelle, a private church-affiliated women's college at New Rochelle, New York, and at Hunter College of the City University of New York, a public college. At that time, Hunter College consisted of two campuses: a co-educational Bronx Campus (now Lehman College of the City University of New York) and a Manhattan women's campus (now co-educational).

The seventy seniors drawn for the study were seeking full-time jobs in accounting, economics, laboratory science, management, marketing, personnel, programming, publishing, research and retailing. Opportunities in these fields were available. Each participating college placement office had job vacancies in these fields reported to them by employers who sought to fill their job vacancies.

Methodology

Because the Placement Readiness Scale had been the most successful in identifying the levels of placement success for each of the three levels of placement readiness, it was used with the Placement Success Scale in this study.

The Chi-Square Test was again the statistical treatment used to test the relationship of high, moderate and low placement readiness to high, moderate and low placement success. It was tested at the 0.05 level of significance and two degrees of freedom.

The Findings

The results of the Chi-Square Test were significant and supported the findings of the first study, indicating that the characteristics of an individual's job-seeking behavior has an effect on success in obtaining a desired job (see Table V). Those with high placement readiness were the most successful in finding employment and those with low placement readiness were unsuccessful. Those with moderate placement readiness tended to gain employment but in a longer period of time than it took those with high placement readiness characteristics.

Therefore, the Placement Readiness Scale successfully identified the levels of placement success for liberal arts seniors seeking positions in business and government, as well as for job seekers in the field of education.

It had been a concern that racial and/or religious prejudice might be an operating factor in hiring practice. The population of this study consisted of Asian, black, Hispanic and white students and reflected the population of the New York Metropolitan area, especially that of New York City. It could also be assumed by employers that students graduating from the two parochial colleges would be of the same religious affiliation as that of the colleges. It might also be assumed that if the employer was of the same faith, he or she might hire these seniors. On the other hand, Hunter College is a public college with a cross section of religions represented in its graduating class.

It was felt that if prejudice was affecting the employment of any of the college populations, a comparison of the percentages of high placement success would reflect this condition. However, where the incidence of

TABLE V

RELATIONSHIP OF PLACEMENT READINESS TO PLACEMENT SUCCESS FOR
LIBERAL ARTS MEN AND WOMEN

Placement Readiness	Placement Success			
	H	M	L	x^2
High	22	11	3	15.164 *p$<$.001
Moderate	1	10	4	8.400 *p$<$.02
Low	0	6	13	13.554 *p$<$.02

*The tabled x^2 at 2df at the .05 level of confidence is 5.991. Since the obtained x^2_2 is greater than the tabled x^2, the results are highly significant. The obtained x^2 is even greater than the tabled x^2 = 13.815 at the .001 level of confidence for the relationship between high placement readiness and high placement success. The obtained x^2 for moderate placement readiness and moderate placement success and for low placement readiness with low placement success was even higher than the tabled x^2 = 7.824 at the .02 level of confidence.

From Nancy D. Stevens, The Relationship of Placement Readiness to Placement Success of Liberal Arts College Students. Unpublished Research Study. Hunter College, 1965.

high placement success was concerned, Iona College had 33 percent of the sample, The College of New Rochelle had 35 percent, and Hunter College had 34 percent. All colleges were virtually equal in the percentage of their seniors who had high placement success. Although the population was not large enough to draw definitive conclusions, it suggested that the individual's job-seeking behavior pattern had more to do with his or her success in gaining employment than did prejudice on the part of the employers.

Formulas of Placement Readiness/Placement Success Relationship

The relationship between the level of placement readiness characteristics and job placement success can be illustrated by the following formulas that show the effect of the style of the job-seeking behavior pattern upon success in procuring a position:

Let:

OP = Job Opportunity
PR_h = High Placement Readiness
PR_m = Moderate Placement Readiness
PR_l = Low Placement Readiness
J_{hs} = Job obtained in short period of time
J_{ms} = Job obtained in longer period of time
$\emptyset$ = Unemployment

Therefore:

(1) High Placement Readiness
     $OP + PR_h = J_{hs}$
(2) Moderate Placement Readiness
     $OP + PR_m = J_{ms}$
(3) Low Placement Readiness
     $OP + PR_l = \emptyset$

THE THIRD STUDY

The relationship of the personality characteristics of independence, dependence, anxiety, sensitivity and neuroticism to levels of placement readiness was the focus of the third study (Schneider and Stevens, 1971; Stevens, 1972, 1973).

Manifestations of maladaptive behavior, as well as personality adjustment, were exhibited and observed in the patterns of job-seeking behavior. The independent, self-actualized behavior of job seekers with high placement readiness indicated effectively adaptive behavior in finding a job, whereas the passive, dependent behavior of low placement readiness (that frequently reflected confusion and conflict) indicated difficulties in personal adjustment that affected the job-seeking process negatively. In addition to these observations, interviewers have frequently suspected that individuals with passive behavior might have anxiety about success as well as failure. This could be a factor that produces a paralyzing effect on an individual's mobilization of personal resources to obtain a job goal. These observations have implications for counseling job seekers in an effort to assist them in increasing the effectiveness of their job-seeking behavior. Consequently, it was important to identify which personality characteristics might be significantly associated with the placement readiness level.

The Design of the Study

The purpose of this study (Schneider and Stevens, 1971) was to test the significant relationship of personality characteristics to the three levels of placement readiness. The focus was on the character dimensions of independence-dependence, anxiety-non-anxiety, depression-cheerfulness, sensitivity-toughmindedness, and neuroticism-non-neuroticism.

Scheier and Cattell's (1961)[1] Neuroticism Sensitivity Scale (NSQ) was selected as a measure of personality characteristics. Its five scales measured sensitivity, depression, dependence, anxiety and a composite score on neuroticism. It also offered independent and combined Sten scores for men and women. The primary thrust of the study was to test the significance of the relationship of measured levels of submissiveness (dependence) and dominance (independence) to identified levels of high, moderate, and low placement readiness as measured by the Placement Readiness Scale.

Population

A random sample of one hundred and fifty graduating seniors, who voluntarily registered with the career counseling and placement offices at the two campuses of Hunter College and the City University of New York, were selected for this study. The population consisted of fifty men and one hundred women and reflected the one-to-two ratio of men to women at the college. This sample was both interracial and interfaith. It was typical of the sophisticated New York City residents who commute to a liberal arts city college.

---

[1]Scheier, Ivan H., and Cattell, Raymond B.: *Handbook for the Neuroticism Scale Questionnaire: "The NSQ."* Copyright 1961 by the Institute for Personality and Ability Testing, Inc. All rights reserved. Adapted and reprinted by permission.

Methodology

At the end of the initial appointment with the career counseling and placement interviewer, the students' responses were evaluated on the Placement Readiness Scale. The students were also given the NSQ to fill out before they left the office.

Placement Readiness Ratings' Reliability

Reliability of the placement readiness ratings was evaluated by an inter-rater evaluation of 25 percent (38) of the seniors interviewed. The seniors were observed and rated by a second staff interviewer during their initial interview, with the permission of the students.

Classes of NSQ Scores

NSQ scores were cut into discrete classes of extremes as follows:

NSQ 8–10 Sten scores represented high anxiety, sensitivity, depression and neuroticism for these respective subscales.

NSQ 1–3 Sten scores represented toughmindedness, cheerfulness, low anxiety and low neuroticism.

Clinical evidence suggested a different variation in grouping for the dominance-submissiveness scale as follows:

NSQ 8–10 Sten scores represented submissiveness.

NSQ 4–7 Sten scores represented true independence.

NSQ 1–3 Sten scores represented counter-dependence.

Methodology

The Chi-Square Test for one degree of freedom and 0.05 level of significance was used. The formula was:

$$x^2 = \frac{N (AD-BC)^2}{(A + B) (C + D) (A + C) (B + D)}$$

The Findings

The reliability of the inter-rater evaluations for the placement readiness ratings was established. There was 100 percent inter-rater agreement, because the interview behavior that was exhibited for high, moderate, and low placement readiness was so clearly identifiable.

The patterns of job-seeking behavior are related to and are a function of the personality dimensions of submissiveness-dominance. High placement readiness is unquestionably associated with true assertiveness and independence, while low placement readiness is unquestionably associated with passivity and dependence (see Table VI).

TABLE VI
PLACEMENT READINESS AND SUBMISSIVENESS-DOMINANCE

Population	Placement Readiness	Passive 8–10	Dominant 4–7	x^2
Men	Low	5	2	11.990 p*<.001
	High	1	17	
Women	Low	9	15	12.500 p*<.001
	High	1	35	
Combined**	Low	12	22	19.221 p*<.001
	High	1	55	

*The tabled x^2 at 1df at .05 level of confidence is 3.841. Since the obtained x^2 is greater than the tabled x^2, the results are highly significant. The results are even higher than the tabled x^2 = 10.827 at the .001 level of confidence.

**Combined numbers do not equal men plus women since combined results were scored and computed at a later date when some original data were no longer available. Combined tables for the NSQ are weighted differently from tables for men and women.

From L. Ronald Schneider and Nancy D. Stevens, Personality characteristics associated with job-seeking behavior patterns. Vocational Guidance Quarterly, 19:194–200, 1971. Copyright AACD. Reprinted with permission.

The dynamics operating in moderate placement readiness are not as clear-cut as would be expected from the previous studies cited above. Individuals exhibiting this behavior seem to be different from those with either high or low placement readiness. When considering the findings in Table VII, there is a reasonably relevant difference for Men and Women Combined between moderate and low placement readiness in relation to passivity and counter-dependence, even though it is not significant at the 0.05 level of significance. However, it should be noted that it is significant at the 0.10 level of significance and, therefore, is in the direction of significance. There was no significant relationship between true independence and counter-dependence for Men and Women Combined and moderate and high placement readiness. Therefore, those job seekers with moderate placement readiness would appear to be more independent and counter-dependent than they would appear to be passive and dependent.

TABLE VII
MODERATE PLACEMENT READINESS AND COUNTER-DEPENDENCE

		Passive 8-10	Dominant 4-7	Counter-dependent 1-3	x^2
Men	High	—	17	8	.007 NS
	Moderate	1	8	4	1.250 NS
	Low	5	—	5	
Women	High	—	35	10	1.863 NS
	Moderate	1	19	11	5.625 *p $<$.02
	Low	9	—	9	
Combined**	High	—	55	11	.255 NS
	Moderate	3	35	9	3.689 *p $<$.10
	Low	12	—	8	

*The tabled x^2 at 1df at the .05 level of confidence is 3.841. Since the obtained x^2 is greater than the tabled x^2, the results are highly significant. The obtained x^2 is even higher than the tabled x^2=5.412 at the .02 level of confidence.

**See note on Table VI.

From L. Ronald Schneider and Nancy D. Stevens, Personality characteristics associated with job-seeking behavior patterns. *Vocational Guidance Quarterly*, 19:194-200, 1971. Copyright AACD. Reprinted with permission.

The essence of the NSQ high sensitivity Sten score, according to Scheier and Cattell (1961), is a helplessness, a gentleness, an impracticality and an idealism that is based on a sensitive intuition. Individuals with high Sten scores tend toward unrealistic goals, and they often have been overprotected and sheltered from the realities of life by an unrealistic home education. The behavior dynamics exhibited in low placement readiness are clearly related to high sensitivity.

The essence of the low NSQ sensitivity Sten score is characterized by a dominant, assertive, aggressive behavior, as well as a toughmindedness, a shrewdness, an objectivity, based on a logical and realistic evaluation of the evidence. High placement readiness is less clearly related to toughmindedness, especially for women. This may be due to the fact that the college population is generally observed to be more sensitive than the general public (see Table VIII).

TABLE VIII
PLACEMENT READINESS AND SENSITIVITY

Placement Readiness		Sensitivity 8-10	1-3	x^2	
Men	Low	2	1	.884	NS
	High	4	7		
Women	Low	14	0	10.572	*p < .005
	High	9	10		
Combined**	Low	17	3	10.031	*p < .005
	High	11	17		

*The tabled x^2=3.841 at 1df and the .05 level of significance. Since the obtained x^2 is greater than the tabled x^2, the results are highly significant. The obtained x^2 is even higher than the tabled x^2=7.879 at the .005 level of confidence.

**See note on Table VI.

From L. Ronald Schneider and Nancy D. Stevens, Personality characteristics associated with job-seeking behavior patterns. *Vocational Guidance Quarterly*, 19:194-200, 1971. Copyright AACD. Reprinted with permission.

Depression and anxiety show no meaningful relationship to levels of placement readiness (see Tables IX–XII). However, a high level of neuroticism was found to be associated with low placement readiness. For a summary of combined scores for men and women, see Table XII.

TABLE IX
PLACEMENT READINESS AND DEPRESSION

	Placement Readiness	Depression		x^2
		8-10	1-3	
Men	Low	1	4	.280 *NS
	High	3	6	
Women	Low	3	13	.090 *NS
	High	3	17	
Combined**	Low	4	11	.066 *NS
	High	6	20	

*The tabled x^2 at 1df at the $.05_3$ level of confidence is 3.841. Inasmuch as the obtained x^2 is less than the tabled x^2, the results are not significant.

**See note on Table VI.

TABLE X
PLACEMENT READINESS AND ANXIETY

		Anxiety 8-10	1-3	x^2
Men	Low	1	2	.321 *NS
	High	2	9	
Women	Low	12	3	3.780 *NS
	High	9	10	
Combined**	Low	8	6	1.327 *NS
	High	12	19	

*The tabled x^2 at 1df at the .05 level of confidence is 3.841. Inasmuch as the obtained x^2 is less than the tabled x^2, the results are not significant.

** See note on Table VI.

TABLE XI
PLACEMENT READINESS AND NEUROTICISM

		Neuroticism 8-10	1-3	x^2
Men	Low	2	2	2.000 NS
	High	1	7	
Women	Low	9	5	11.798 *p $<$ .001
	High	0	12	
Combined**	Low	11	5	6.984 *p $<$ .01
	High	6	17	

*The tabled x^2 at 1df at the .05 level of confidence is 3.841. Inasmuch as the obtained x^2 is greater than the tabled x^2, the results are highly significant.

**See note on Table VI.

TABLE XII
RELATIONSHIP OF PERSONALITY CHARACTERISTICS TO LEVELS OF
PLACEMENT READINESS
MEN AND WOMEN COMBINED**

Personality Characteristics	Placement Readiness		
	H	L	x^2
Submissiveness- dominance	1 55	12 22	19.221 *p $<$ .001
Sensitivity- tough-mindedness	11 17	17 3	10.031 *p $<$ .005
Neuroticism- non-neuroticism	6 17	11 5	6.984 *p $<$ .01
Anxiety- non-anxiety	12 19	8 6	1.327 NS
Depression- cheerfulness	6 20	11 4	.066 NS

*The tabled x^2 at 1df at the .05 level of confidence is 3.841. Inasmuch as the obtained x^2 is greater than the tabled x^2, the results are highly significant.

**See note on Table VI.

SUMMARY

1. Three patterns of job-seeking behavior were identified: (a) those job seekers with high placement readiness had crystallized job goals and were independent and capable of mobilizing their personal resources in seeking a job; (b) those with low placement readiness had vague goals and were dependent, passive, and they appeared frequently to be floundering; and (c) those with moderate placement readiness exhibited a mixture of the characteristics of both high and low placement readiness and they were actively exploring.

2. Job seekers with the characteristics of high placement readiness obtained desired jobs in the shortest period of time, even in a very poor labor market. Those with the characteristics of moderate placement

readiness obtained desired jobs, but it took them a longer period of time to do so than it did those with high placement readiness. Those with the characteristics of low placement readiness did not obtain desired jobs, even when there were many job opportunities in the labor market.

3. The Placement Readiness Scale was the most effective scale in its ability to predict the success of job seekers in obtaining a job by means of the identification of their level of placement readiness. It was not only effective with job seekers who were professionally trained in education, but it was also successful with liberal arts graduating seniors seeking positions in business and government.

4. Patterns of job-seeking behavior are a function of character structure rather than emotionality. Depression and anxiety are not related to the levels of placement readiness, but high neuroticism is related to low placement readiness. High sensitivity, which is characterized by helplessness, impracticality and an unrealistic home environment, is also related to low placement readiness.

5. The personality dimension of submissiveness-dominance is associated with placement readiness. Dominance is clearly associated with high placement readiness and submissiveness with low placement readiness.

6. Behaviorally, moderate placement readiness is different from the behaviors that are characteristic of either high or low placement readiness. However, the men and women with moderate placement readiness tend to exhibit more of the characteristics of high placement readiness than they do the low placement readiness characteristics.

7. The levels of placement readiness reflect a continuum of developmental job-seeking behavior. Job goals tend to become increasingly defined and specific, and the exhibited behavior becomes more independent and self-actualized.

The following three chapters focus on the personality dynamics of the positive (high placement readiness), negative (low placement readiness) and the transitional (moderate placement readiness) job-seeking behavior patterns. Aspects of the social environment that affect the development of personality and life-style are discussed for each job-seeking behavior pattern.

Chapter Three

POSITIVE JOB-SEEKING BEHAVIOR

The style of individuals who readily find jobs is characterized by specific and crystallized career goals, as well as by assertive, independent and self-actualized behavior. This is the most effective job-seeking behavior pattern because of the positive-oriented focus on obtaining a desired job. A mobilization of their personal resources toward their goals appears to be in operation.

In the initial research study cited in Chapter Two, these characteristics were identified as high placement readiness, because the job seekers who exhibited them obtained desired jobs in the shortest period of time when compared to the other two groups of job seekers who exhibited different styles of behavior. Placement counselors who interviewed them sensed that they were ready for job placement, and employers also responded positively to them by offering employment.

DYNAMICS

This chapter explores some of the personal dynamics that contribute to the development of the positive job-seeking behavior pattern. The individual's perceptions, self-concept and family social environment are discussed in terms of their contributions to the underlying development of the realistic, independent, self-actualized job seeker who has crystallized and specific job goals.

Perception of Family Environment

Generalized postulations of personality dynamics were formulated by Rogers (1951), some aspects of which may be used as a basis for understanding the behavior dynamics of the positive job-seeking behavior pattern. He theorized that the organism, as he stated it, reacts to reality as it is perceived and that there is a basic tendency for the organism to move toward actualizing, maintaining or enhancing itself. Consequently, behavior is the goal-oriented attempt to satisfy needs as they are experienced and as they are perceived. The individual's perceptions of reality are the critical factor in determining his or her behavior.

Perception of one's evolving social experiences, even in the early years, tends to set the scene for the development of future attitudes and behavior regarding self, vocational choices, job-seeking behavior and work. How the family environment is perceived by the individual can have a critical effect. A supportive family milieu provides the environment in which developmental tasks that need to be coped with from early childhood through adolescence can be learned by the individual. This learning process contributes to the individual's personality development, concept of self, social adaptation and job-seeking behavior.

Erikson's Stages of Development

Erikson (1950) has identified and defined the stages of development and the tasks associated with them for the different ages from infancy through the adult years. The first five of these stages are discussed below as a framework for understanding the early foundation of the personality dynamics of job seekers with the positive job-seeking behavior pattern.

Erikson's first stage is that of *Trust vs. Basic Mistrust*, which covers the first year of life. This is the period during which the infant senses the evident acceptance of a caring and nurturing mother who will respond warmly to his or her needs. Because her acceptance is felt, the child develops a feeling of trust from this relationship so that attitudes of trust begin to evolve.

This is also the period in which a child's perceptions of his or her social experience within the family begin to take form and shape a concept of self. In this caring and supportive environment, the infant perceives himself or herself to be loved and to be valued. Perceptions tend to be accurately symbolized and become the foundation upon which a strong self-concept is formed.

A sense of independence develops in the second stage, *Autonomy vs. Shame and Doubt*, around the ages of one-and-a-half to three years. As the mother gives encouragement and supportive action to her child's effort to crawl and to walk, the child senses her pleasure as these skills are accomplished. Consequently, the child develops a sense of ability, power and autonomy as his or her efforts to develop new skills are accomplished and are positively reinforced by the mother's evident pleasure.

The pleasure principle of learning is in operation and it reinforces these early attempts to be independent and to make an effort to try. The roots of the independent behavior exhibited by individuals with positive job-seeking behavior are based in this early supportive relationship.

Erikson's third stage of *Initiative vs. Guilt* is the period from about the ages of three to six, during which the individuals with positive job-seeking behavior would have begun to develop initiative. This would be the expected mode of behavior to evolve from the independence that has been developing. In a sense, it is the root of the self-actualizing behavior that is exhibited when they seek employment.

The *Industry vs. Inferiority* developmental stage from the age of six to the start of puberty is a critical period in the development of attitudes toward work which can affect behavior exhibited in the job-seeking process, as well as behavior on the job that is procured. This is the time when the individual begins to develop either an orientation toward or an alienation to work.

When the child enters school and becomes part of a cooperative, productive enterprise, he or she also becomes involved in a new and broader socialization process. In this new environment, it is a learning experience to have to subordinate personal wishes and desires and to sublimate them for other pleasures that may be more acceptable to the group at large, be it the class or the entire school. The child also becomes aware of new opportunities outside the home environment that begin to mold him or her. New personal abilities are discovered. New tasks are learned. New skills are developed. It is also discovered that tasks have to be completed and that people in authority have expectations concerning his or her performance in class.

When the child is successful in coping with these new tasks, good workmanship develops. Tasks begin to be mastered outside the home environment and work begins to develop meaning. A positive response to these new experiences in the school setting is a key factor in enabling the person to become work oriented.

The stage of *Identity vs. Role Diffusion* follows and covers the period of adolescence. For individuals who have positive job-seeking behavior, this would be the time during which they begin to explore their interests, abilities, values and skills in an attempt to understand themselves better and to identify possible career directions. This is traditionally so where men are concerned and has become increasingly so for women, who traditionally have focused on their future in terms of marriage and family but who currently consider a career as a viable option. It is a time when future goals are considered in terms of the past and present. This involves a synthesis of how they perceive themselves and their awareness of the expectations that significant others may have for them.

Effect of Family Environment

Another study by Stevens and Schneider (1967a) investigated the role that family dynamics can play in the formation of job-seeking behavior. An in-depth analysis was made of the clinical data that was obtained on eighteen Hunter College seniors who were receiving personal counseling from the college psychologist and who were also seeking employment with the help of the Career Counseling and Placement Office at the Bronx Campus.

The population was evaluated by the Placement Readiness Scale to ascertain the level of placement readiness for each senior. The college psychologist identified the patterns of family dynamics that were the essence of their family environment. Both the placement counselor and the psychologist saw this special population on a continuous basis for six months. Consequently, the subjects saw each investigator a minimum of four or five times.

It was found that the young adults who had the positive job-seeking behavior pattern tended to have grown up in a family environment in which they received encouragement in trying new experiences, developing their abilities and interests and in making their own choices. They also received emotional support from both of their parents.

This family environment not only presented opportunities for identification with the appropriate family figure but also provided a positive and supportive relationship with the parent of the opposite sex. Fathers played a warm, positive role in the lives of their children. They, in turn, were admired and were viewed as successful in the opinion of the family members and in terms of whatever success meant to these individuals.

Mothers, whose main responsibility was to raise the children, were caring, consistent and supportive within the family circle, regardless of any outside work commitments that they may have had. They contributed to a nurturing family milieu. Both parents provided positive role models to whom their children could relate.

Supportive parental behavior is a critical factor in the early period of childhood for the personality development of the individual. Bordin (1965) has indicated that this supportive quality is necessary for an individual to develop behavior which is free from anxiety and from the need to be defensive. He states that "the more the individual is supported by the nurturant actions of others during his early stages of extreme helplessness and the more he is encouraged to make use of his developing resources, the more he will turn to his own achievements as a possible escape from helplessness."

Consequently, it is this dynamic of emotional support in the social environment of those with the positive job-seeking behavior pattern that has laid the foundation for the incidence of cheerfulness, dominance, toughmindedness and low level of neuroticism that Schneider and Stevens (1971) found to be associated with the high placement readiness group of college seniors in their research on the personality characteristics associated with the levels of placement readiness.

As a result of the interaction between the individual and his or her social environment, a consistent concept of self is developed, because experiences are perceived and symbolized accurately and are organized and assimilated into the self-structure. This process leads to adaptive, realistic behavior and psychological adjustment. Behavior is consistent with the individual's self-concept, and, as a result, basic attitudes about self are reflected in social and vocational situations.

Development of the Self-Concept

Super (1951) also identifies childhood as the period of time when self-concepts are formed. They evolve as a result of the children's wide range of contact with adults and friends, as well as through the many social activities, class activities and exposures to the different academic subjects.

Consequently, their concepts of self are stable in adolescence and in adulthood. Super feels that the adolescents' exploratory efforts tend to "clarify, elaborate upon, and confirm the concept of self which has already begun to emerge and to crystallize."

Super (1951) has defined a self-concept to be "the product of interaction between inherited aptitudes . . . glandular factors affecting physical energy, opportunity in the form of chances to observe and try out a given type of activity with a given kind of competition, and impressions of the extent to which the results of trying something meet with the approval of superiors and fellows." Super (1963)[1] later defined it as "a picture of the self in some role, some situation, in a position, performing some set of functions, or in some web of relationships."

Metadimensions of the Self-Concepts

Super (1963) also identified as metadimensions of the self-concepts seven trait characteristics that people use to describe themselves. These are self-esteem, clarity, abstraction, refinement, certainty, stability and realism. Many of these are revealed in the interview responses of job seekers with the positive job-seeking behavior pattern. These job seekers give evidence of having developed strong self-concepts.

Self-Esteem. When job seekers feel themselves to be worthy and successful, their self-esteem is reflected in their job-seeking behavior. In the interview, they state positively their qualifications for employment in the job they seek.

For example:

> "I was successful in problem solving when I was put in charge of the office for three months this past year . . . when the office manager was taken ill . . . and I know that I can do a good job getting people to work on a team basis. I pulled it off because I'm good at directing people."

This statement reflects the metadimension of self-esteem based on the job seeker's assessment of her work experience. It is clear that her self-knowledge and the outcome of her work efforts in a time of crisis have reinforced her positive feelings about herself.

Clarity. Job seekers with the positive behavior pattern reflect more clarity of self-concept than those with the transitional or negative behavior pattern. There does seem to be a sharp awareness of the importance of related experience to meeting the qualifications of a job they desire. They seem to recognize that they are differentiated from others when in competition for the same job. It is illustrated by the following:

> "I know I want a job that is people-focused rather than, say, data-focused. It's important to me that the job be more in a service area than in business. I'm thinking that my background might lend itself

---

[1]From Super, Donald E.: *Career Development: Self Concept Theory* (New York: College Entrance Examination Board, 1963). Reprinted by permission. Copyright 1963 by the College Entrance Examination Board.

to settlement house work or community service work. I've had three years' work in recreation and four years' in group counseling of youth with addiction problems, which gives me a breadth of experience not every one can offer."

In this instance, the job seeker indicates that he has defined what work he wants to do and has related it to the experience he has obtained which also supports his application for such work.

Another example is this statement:

"Why should you hire me? . . . Well . . . because I am a problem solver and a risk taker. I can make decisions, and it seems to me that you need someone who likes to do these things and who can get along with people, too. That is why I want a job in management."

Certainty. These statements also seem to reflect the metadimension of certainty. No qualifying adjectives are present that detract from their work experience. These positive, definite statements that describe themselves suggest that there is little doubt that these job seekers know who they are, what they want to do, and that they are making an effective presentation in an effort to have the opportunity to do it.

Realism. Placement counselors have considered job seekers with the positive job-seeking behavior pattern to be reality oriented. Super's (1963)[2] metadimension of "Realism of the self concepts denotes the degree of agreement between the individual's picture of himself and external, objective evidence of his status on the characteristics in question."

Empirically, the job seeker who sought a helping people-type job pictured himself in the nurturing role of the social service aide or counselor. The job goal appeared to be reality oriented in that he had had related experience in appropriate settings that not only may have reinforced his concept of self in this role but which also was related to the job requirements of work in his desired field.

Another stated:

"I am an accounting major, and I've had two years experience as a bookkeeper and a part-time job this past spring in the college's accounting office. I think I am in good shape for an accounting job in a small or medium size CPA firm. My grades aren't quite good

---

[2]From Super, Donald E.: *Career Development: Self Concept Theory* (New York: College Entrance Examination Board, 1963). Reprinted by permission. Copyright 1963 by the College Entrance Examination Board.

enough for the 'Big Eight,' but they're good enough to qualify me for consideration in other firms."

This second job seeker also gives evidence that her job goal was realistic. Her information about job requirements and about her strengths has been accurately perceived and assimilated. This is suggested by the fact that she adjusted her job goal to small and medium size firms rather than to the prominent CPA firms due to their entry job requirement of top grades.

Only four of Super's metadimensions of self-concepts have been discussed in terms of their effect on the individual's positive job-seeking behavior. The functions of self-esteem, clarity, certainty and realism have been focused upon because their effects can be more readily observed in interview behavior by the placement counselor than can the meta-dimensions of abstraction, refinement and stability. These have been empirical observations and have not been formally measured and tested. Nevertheless, they present a clue for future research in terms of Super's self-concept theory on the role of metadimensions of self-concepts of job seekers interviewed by placement counselors.

Case Studies

Typical of many individuals with the positive-oriented job-seeking behavior pattern is the graduating senior with a history major who, in her initial interview with her placement counselor, expressed an interest in programming. She indicated that she had elective credits in program-ming courses that totalled up to more than a minor and had done an internship for one semester in a programming department of a company. She had found these courses and the work in the internship interesting, regretting that she had discovered the field too late in her academic career to be able to change her major to computer science. Therefore, she did the next best thing and that was to take as many elective credits in programming as she was able to do.

She indicated flexibility. If she could not get a job in a company computer training program, then she thought she would apply to a college computer science department for entry into a special program of courses that would enable her to increase her chances to obtain such a job. She planned to contact the companies from which the placement interviewer had received entry job openings. She also planned to contact the companies that the interviewer identified as having training programs. She already had left her application at several personnel offices, including the one in the company where she had had an internship. Although independent in her efforts to get a job, she felt free to seek and to use the specific help of the placement office to extend her campaign.

Another job seeker was a college graduate with a master's degree in business administration who had been working for eight years in business. She had held a job in middle management for the past five years. She had developed good skills, of which she was cognizant, and she was direct in her approach and assertive in her behavior. She felt that she probably had gone as far as she could where she was currently employed, and she wanted to see what else she could do, perhaps in another setting like education.

She also wanted to reassess herself at this moment in time. After having taken several test exercises that gave her and the counselor a pattern of her interests, values, skills and meaningful activities, she recognized that the data confirmed her present position in management as being the best career fit for her. However, she was not totally content with this news because she felt that something was missing and she was able to identify the problem. She did not have an opportunity to be creative in developing her own program.

She began to explore the occupational literature for information about administrative positions in education and in foundations.

When she returned to see the counselor, she indicated that she had an idea for training staff that might lend itself to an educational setting, but she was uncertain how to approach colleges and educational foundations about it. She elaborated on her plans in some detail. Her idea was logically presented and well thought through. The counselor asked her why she never had discussed it within her management group and asked if it was something that would be a contribution to the functioning of her department unit. She was surprised at this suggestion.

When she returned for her next appointment, she stated that she had decided to stay in her current job, because in reviewing her idea she saw how it could be adapted for business and she intended to discuss it with the head of her department within a few days.

This was a career woman who was successfully established in her work who desired to explore and assess her ennui and her professional options. She exhibited a self-understanding that was confirmed by the exercises she took. She exhibited assertive, self-actualized behavior in exploring an outlet for a professional plan that she devised.

Schema of Positive Job-Seeking Behavior

The dynamic process of the positive-oriented job-seeking behavior pattern (Stevens, 1962; Stevens and Schneider, 1967a) can be diagrammed as follows:

> Needs → Fantasy Goals → Uncertainty → Exploration of Opportunities → Evaluation of External and Internal Factors → Narrowing of Options to Tentative Choices → Compromise → Crystallization of Career or Work Field Goal → Specification of Realistic Job Goal Within Chosen Field of Work

It is assumed that individuals with this particular job-seeking behavior pattern have self-actualizing needs that can be expressed in work, and that work becomes increasingly meaningful if these needs are met. Whatever these needs are for any given individual, they first would produce fantasy goals. For the individuals who have perceived and symbolized social experience accurately, fantasy seems to be used as a tryout vehicle in the mind's theatrical stage. It is a device for imagining themselves in different roles, as well as for imagining how it feels to be doing different kinds of work. It is also a means by which plans for achieving a new goal may be formulated. It serves as an economical means for exploring the ramifications of a course of action before the activity is actually put to the test in practice.

Exploration of job options is pursued, together with a consideration of internal and external factors. This can mean information about a variety of possible options, as well as self-knowledge about skills, abilities, limitations, values, family responsibilities, family feelings and their economic situation, etc. The evaluation process that follows involves assessing and balancing the external factors collected about the options under consideration together with the internal factors of such knowledge. A compromise frequently results from such an evaluation in the sense of their working out a "near best fit" between the job goal that the job seekers desire and the jobs that are possible for them to obtain. Such a compromise often appears to be a "near best fit" to their desired job goals, so that the jobs that they procure may become the alternate stepping stones that can provide advancement for them in the career direction that they have chosen. They demonstrate adaptive behavior in seeking a job.

These considerations lead to crystallization of a career field that is realistic for the individual and finally to the identification of a specific position or positions in the field that the job seeker desires.

SUMMARY

Job seekers with the positive job-seeking behavior pattern have crystallized, specific, realistic job goals. They also exhibit independent, self-actualized behavior, which is a function of their dominance, tough-mindedness and low level of neuroticism.

Their early social experience tends to be accurately perceived, so that they develop trust, independence, initiative, industriousness and a strong self-concept.

Their family environment is supportive, so that they have an opportunity to learn from their mistakes, explore and test new situations and make decisions.

Chapter Four

NEGATIVE JOB-SEEKING BEHAVIOR

The negative job-seeking behavior pattern is the style exhibited by job seekers who are unsuccessful in obtaining a job. This is the pattern in which job seekers exhibit vague and confused job goals with passive, dependent and floundering behavior. They tend not to procure any job at all, let alone one that they may desire. These job seekers appear to be incapable of mobilizing their personal resources toward a solution of their vocational problems, and they seem to expect others to give them direction. In the initial research cited in Chapter Two, these characteristics were identified as low placement readiness because the placement counselors who interviewed these job seekers sensed that they were unready for job placement. Employers responded to them in a similar manner to that of the placement counselors. They did not offer them jobs.

DYNAMICS

The crux of the problem in getting a job for these individuals with negative job-seeking behavior is their lack of crystallized job goals and their passive, dependent behavior. Schneider and Stevens (1971) found that this type of behavior is a function of their submissiveness and sensitivity character dimensions discussed in Chapter Two. Their job-seeking behavior is characterized by passivity and helplessness.

Another finding that undoubtedly contributes to their ineffective job-seeking behavior is their significantly high neuroticism level. However, anxiety and depression are not significantly related to job-seeking behavior. This indicates that negative job-seeking behavior is less affected by immediate emotionality than it is by character structure. On the other hand, placement interviewers do recognize anxiety and depression in their interviewees. Schneider and Stevens (1971) felt that such incidences of emotionality indicated that high levels of anxiety could be related to high levels of sensitivity, dependence and neuroticism which are more likely to be found in those individuals with negative job-seeking behavior than would be found in those with either the positive or transitional job-seeking behavior pattern. Further research is necessary to test this possible relationship.

Erikson's Stages of Development

Erikson's (1950) stages of developmental tasks provide a basis for understanding how the perception of individuals tends to be formed by their social experiences. Using his stages of development as a framework, the tasks of childhood and adolescence are interpolated by the author in terms of their development and effect upon job seekers with the negative pattern of job-seeking behavior.

Erikson indicated that the first stage is that of *Trust vs. Basic Mistrust* (covering ages from one to one and one-half), which is the time when the infant senses either the acceptance and caring or the rejection and annoyance of the adult taking care of him or her. During this period the child's first awareness of the social environment is through the cues that are perceived from the physical contact with the mother. Physical cues, such as the possible abruptness of the mother's gestures, even the possible quickening of her heartbeats as the child is held in her arms when she is interrupted from her own activities in order to take care of his or her needs, may be interpreted as annoyance by the infant, whether or not it is an accurate perception of the situation. The child may also yell to get relief from discomfort and sense the mother's annoyance with these distress calls.

Consequently, a sense of mistrust develops. A mistrust of the adult who is looking after the child's needs can occur because of a seeming lack of concern. Mistrust of self also can develop because of the sense of being powerless and helpless in the attempt to get what is needed or desired. This is the period of time when perceptions of self first take shape, and in this particular family environment a poor self-concept begins to be formed. The sense of being unworthy of love and attention can later be seen in the job-seeking adult as self-debasement, lack of self-worth and low self-esteem.

Autonomy vs. Shame and Doubt (ages one and one-half to three) follows. The behavior of individuals with the characteristics of negative job-seeking behavior is rooted in this stage of development. In this period a sense of self-doubt, helplessness and shame tends to develop rather than the feelings of ability, power and autonomy that those with the positive job-seeking behavior pattern tend to perceive about themselves. This is the period when the child begins to crawl and walk, reaches out to explore things on low tables and starts to babble incoherently, all of which require increased time on the part of the mother for supervision. As the child's exhibited behavior becomes increasingly active and exploratory, the mother's annoyance can increase by these additional intrusions that are made on her time.

Her irritation tends to be sensed by the child, whose feelings of mistrust and personal inadequacy begin to be confirmed and reinforced. Feelings of doubt develop as the child perceives that he or she is incapable of bringing pleasure and pride to a significant other. As this perception of the parent's reaction to exploratory physical activities continues, self-doubt is reinforced.

Initiative vs. Guilt is Erikson's third stage of development that covers the years from three to six. This is the period when other siblings may be born into the family. Jealousy over mother's attention to the younger children is the usual reaction. Should parental support be withdrawn too quickly from the older child within this period of time, guilt feelings concerning his or her jealousy ensue and feelings of inferiority are reinforced. The individual feels that he or she cannot appeal to others.

The pace of withdrawal of parental support is a key factor. According to Bordin (1965):

> It would seem that high parental commitment during the first year or two is crucial to the avoidance of an overtly dependent reaction to dependency anxiety. Parents who accelerate the pace of withdrawal of commitment after the first two years, breaking its cadence with the developing resources of the child, are likely to contribute to the development of the counter-dependent pattern of behavior.

Hostile behavior toward the dominating parent tends to evolve. Consequently, the passivity and dependence of job seekers with negative job-seeking behavior have roots in the very early experiences of the individual's childhood.

The *Industry vs. Inferiority* stage occurs within the age range of six to ten and is the period when attitudes toward work begin to be formed that can affect the individual's job-seeking behavior as well as his or her attitude toward work. Rather than develop an orientation toward work, feelings of inferiority further develop for the individual who has grown up in this family milieu. When the child enters school, he or she has the opportunity to learn new skills outside the home. If the child is unable to learn such skills as subordinating his or her wishes to the greater need of the group, conforming to what is expected and successfully coping with content of class subjects, the child can feel incapable of mastering problems that arise in school with classwork and classmates. Consequently, feelings of inferiority can become entrenched. When he or she does not achieve in school, then work becomes a chore rather than a meaningful and satisfying activity.

When experiences in school tend to reinforce the feelings of self-doubt and powerlessness that have already evolved from perceived family experiences, individuals tend not to become task oriented. In job-seeking behavior, their goals are not apt to be related to work or career as a meaningful activity that brings personal satisfaction. For some, work fields that are perceived by individuals as having status in the eyes of a significant other may be focused upon as a desirable goal for that reason alone, rather than because of the potential satisfaction that may be derived from performing the work tasks in these given fields.

For others, work becomes a means of earning a living and often is regarded by them as *just a job*. Work may also be seen as a means of attaining the money to obtain things that will bring possible pleasure. Consequently, any type of work to be performed may be unimportant. Therefore, when seeking a job the individual's job goal may not be clearly specified and may even be vague. "Get me a job . . . any job" may well be all the job seeker desires. However, this type of response reflects the personal dynamics that contribute to the negative results of the job seeker's efforts when competing for jobs in the labor market.

Identity vs. Role Diffusion is the fifth stage which occurs from ages ten to twenty and is the end of childhood. The adolescent from this constricting family environment tends not to have a sense of identity. The person who has perceived himself or herself to be unloved from early social experiences has developed a sense of mistrust of his or her own ability to be loved, as well as a doubt about his or her capabilities to attain what is desired and a feeling of inferiority regarding his or her accomplishments. The family environment as perceived is not supportive in encouraging and enabling the individual to develop skills, so that self-confidence to explore and to test is lacking. As a result, there is a limited and negative sense of identity at best.

Consequently, there is confusion about what to be in the world of work, which is generally considered during this stage of development. It is not surprising that these individuals with the negative job-seeking behavior pattern are confused and vague about job goals, and are passive and dependent in their attempts to identify a job goal that they should seek.

Effect of Family Environment

In an in-depth study of the family environment of a special population of college seniors seeking employment, Stevens and Schneider (1967a) found that those seniors with the negative job-seeking behavior pattern had a family milieu whose dynamics were virtually opposite to those of the individuals with the positive job-seeking behavior described in Chapter Three. Fathers were passive and ineffectual in the family group. They were generally considered to be hopeless failures by other members of the family. Some of the sons in the research group referred to their fathers as "disgusting failures," with a strong, vehement tone in their voice. Mothers were dominant and aggressive. They held high hopes and had driving ambitions for their children, especially for their sons. They also exhibited overprotective attitudes towards their children.

The effect of this family social environment upon the individual was the development of the tendency to become increasingly dependent, resentful, constricted and repressed in expressing assertiveness, aggressiveness and feelings of hostility. There were pathogenic factors operating in this social environment that affected the perception and personality development of the individuals growing up in this milieu.

Stevens and Schneider further found that these job seekers did not have a crystallized sense of identity; they were confused. Having grown up in a constricted family environment that was not supportive, they had neither tested things out for themselves, nor had they felt free to learn from making mistakes, nor had they found out what they themselves felt and valued.

It was found that there was a tendency for these individuals to assume the values and goals of the dominant parent as their own. This was due not only to the dependent relationship that had evolved but also to their own sense of inferiority and need for approval from that parent. The fear of being considered as hopeless a failure as their fathers motivated their approach toward the dominant parent's attitudes, values and goals without testing them for themselves. Consequently, in a very real sense, their personal and vocational development was stunted.

Development of the Self-Concept

Super (1951) indicated that an individual's self-concept is formed in the early years of childhood, so that what may be discovered by exploration during adolescence is not a discovery of something new about himself or herself but a discovery of something that is already there. Consequently, in the case of the individual with negative job-seeking behavior, social experience is distorted and perceived in such a manner that mistrust, self-doubt and guilt, feelings of inferiority and confusion ensue. Maladaptive behavior results from these distorted perceptions which affect the manner in which a person seeks a job. In the case of the job seeker with negative job-seeking behavior, it is with passive, dependent, confused and floundering behavior that the individual seeks a job. The roots of such behavior can be found in the individual's perception of his or her early social environment, as well as in some of the pathogenic factors that also operate in this family milieu.

As a result, these individuals exhibiting the negative job-seeking behavior pattern have developed poor self-concepts. Self-concepts and attitudes are reflected in their responses during the interview, and the placement counselor becomes aware of the characteristics of the interviewees' behavior.

Metadimensions of the Self-Concepts

Super's (1963) metadimensions of the self-concepts provide the characteristics of traits which were described in Chapter Three. Again, the metadimensions of self-esteem, clarity, certainty and realism are four of the seven metadimensions or characteristics that can be identified in the interview responses of the placement interviewer. The lack of them can also be recognized.

Self-Esteem. Generally, these job seekers tend to give the impression that they do not hold themselves in much self-esteem. The reason for this may be that they tend not to mention any abilities and accomplishments. When they are asked about skills, abilities and accomplishments, they tend to describe them with qualifying phrases that dismiss them as being unimportant.

For example, one woman said: "Yes . . . I was asked to head the Bazaar Committee, but . . . that was only volunteer work. Anyone could have done it."

Another stated: "My job is just a clerical one. I helped out in the office . . . like when the office manager was sick, but I only did it until she came back." She did not see the value of this experience.

Clarity. Super (1963)[1] defines clarity of the self-concept as the "awareness of the nature of attributes. . . . " This is a characteristic that is not found in individuals with the negative pattern of job-seeking behavior who tend to speak of themselves and their job goals in vague terms, which furthers the impression that they do not know themselves well and do not have a clear picture of themselves. It is frequently noted by placement interviewers that they are unable to identify such attributes as their interests, abilities or skills and that they are unaware of their strengths and weaknesses.

For example, one man stated: "I don't know what I want to do. . . . I really don't have any skills . . . or abilities. . . . "

Another job seeker replied: "How can you help me? Get me a job . . . any job will do that is interesting. Tell me, do you have an interesting job on file? . . . I'll take it!"

A woman stated: "I really don't have any experience. No skills. I'm only a housewife going to college . . . because my husband thought I might find myself . . . what I want to do. You know, I don't know what I'm interested in . . . I don't have any skills or anything."

She did not recognize that by successfully managing a home while attending college classes she had developed skills that could be translated for the world of work.

These individuals also are unaware of their job options in the labor market, and they appear to be floundering about what they want to do. Clarity is related to having vocational preferences, and it is understandable why these job seekers seem to be casting about for someone to make these decisions for them.

In the case of these job seekers, there is no evidence that they confidently attribute traits to themselves as do those job seekers with the positive job-seeking behavior pattern. In fact, they seem to be unable to describe themselves because, as has been noted above, they do not understand themselves.

Certainty. The metadimension of certainty is another characteristic that is lacking in job seekers with negative job-seeking behavior. They express job goals in vague terms because they are uncertain of their interests,

---

[1]From Super, Donald E.: *Career Development: Self Concept Theory* (New York: College Entrance Examination Board, 1963). Reprinted by permission. Copyright 1963 by the College Entrance Examination Board.

abilities and skills. In fact, their attributes frequently appear to be unknown to them. This is illustrated by the housewife attending college who did not recognize that she had life skills that had enabled her to keep her home running while attending college. Instead, she felt she had nothing upon which to base a choice of career direction. She also did not seem to have an understanding regarding the relationship of such attributes to work and job goals. This frequently is the case.

For example, one man stated: "I'm looking for a job . . . any kind of job . . . something that's good."

Frequently, upon questioning, it is revealed that the interviewees seek out the suggestions of other persons, rather than make their own decisions, because they do not seem to know what kind of job they really want.

For example, one woman said: "Professor W said I should get a job near home, and he told me to try personnel work. What do you think?"

Another job seeker asked: "What kind of a job should I try to get? I don't know . . . you know about so many different jobs."

Realism. Super's (1963)[2] metadimension of realism "of the self concepts denotes the degree of agreement between the individual's picture of himself, and external, objective evidence of his status on the characteristics in question." It has already been noted that some job seekers with the characteristics of the negative job-seeking behavior pattern (low placement readiness in Chapter Two) have adopted job goals that strongly reflect wish fulfillment and unreality. This seems to occur when the desired goal has been identified without any reality factors coming into the consideration of the choice. It tends to happen when individuals are unaware of their personal traits and seem to be too passive to identify these traits and explore their relationship to career options.

A sophomore stated: "I'm a psychology student and I want a job doing therapy. . . . I can start any time because I'm not finishing the term if you get it for me."

Another job seeker said: "My grades in accounting are average . . . about a C. My mother thinks I'm right not to consider anything but the 'Big Eight' CPA firms. That's where the money and the prestige are. . . . I . . . uh . . . want to know if you have any vacancies from them that I could apply for."

---

[2]From Super, Donald E.: *Career Development: Self Concept Theory* (New York: College Entrance Examination Board, 1963). Reprinted by permission. Copyright 1963 by the College Entrance Examination Board.

No consideration of the employers' requirements is given by these job seekers. The fact that they do not meet such requirements is ignored.

Case Study

The case study presented below is drawn from Stevens and Schneider's (1967a) research study on the effect of the family environment on job-seeking behavior dynamics.

Bert went to the placement office in his senior year at the suggestion of his mother. He was confused about what he wanted to do. He had majored in economics with a minor in psychology, hoping that by studying psychology he could understand himself better. He was unable to identify his own interests, values, strengths and limitations, let alone able to explore career goals based on these inner factors. He indicated that his mother wanted him to be a stockbroker because stockbrokers made good money. Although he had done poorly in his finance courses, he thought he would like to try it, nevertheless. He said he felt that he could not do well in his studies because he could not concentrate due to free-floating thoughts. He could not sleep because he worried about what people meant by what they said to him.

Because of these revelations that indicated to the placement counselor that there might well be signs of pathology present, a referral was made to the college clinical psychologist who could help Bert to see what was troubling him. Bert accepted the referral after saying that he really needed his sleep. After seeing the psychologist a few times, Bert returned to his placement counselor to say that he felt unready for job placement counseling. During this interview he recognized that he was reacting emotionally. He recognized also that he should discuss his reaction with the psychologist. No further contact was had with Bert until after he had graduated, when he dropped in to say that he would be joining the Navy in order to have more time to think about his career decisions. He hoped that he would be lucky enough to like the training that the Navy assigned to him. He added, "I just might have that career problem worked out for me, so that I could follow it in civilian life, too."

From the view of the placement counselor this was a person who was so passive, dependent and confused that he was joining the Navy to delay the process of having to make a career decision and, by so doing, possibly have the Navy make it for him by assigning him to a special training that might also be applicable to civilian work. The fact that he offered the reason for going to see the placement counselor was his mother's suggestion also indicated his dependence. He went as he had been told to do. However, he would not make any effort to explore his values and interests, strengths and limitations. He could not actually participate in the career counseling relationship. His self-concept was poor; to look at himself might have been too threatening. He avoided looking at himself by joining the Navy with the explanation that it gave him more time to think things through.

On the other hand, when he mentioned that his mother wanted him to become a stockbroker, he readily admitted that he did not do well in the essential finance courses. On the face of it, the career field seemed to be unrealistic. One might assume that he did not have the ability to grasp the course content, but this was contradicted by the fact that he had done fairly well in related economic courses. It also seemed possible that his poor grades in finance courses might have been a way to punish his parent for pressuring him even though he sought her advice.

There was possibly another agenda for his visit to the placement counselor, which in the eyes of his classmates was not an unusual thing for a senior to do. He mentioned troubled thoughts that broke into his concentration and into his ability to sleep because of his focusing on what other people meant when they spoke to him. It was possible by mentioning these experiences that he might be referred to the psychologist's office for personal help. If this was the result of his placement interview, it was easier for him to say, "The placement counselor said that I should see you" than to enter that office and make an appointment on his own initiative. The fact that the placement counselor was of the same gender as the dominating parent, and not that of the more submissive parent with whom he could not associate, could have made this possible manipulation to get personal help easier for him to try as a strategy.

Bert was seen three times for personal counseling. During the first interview with the psychologist he admitted immediately that he felt inadequate and unconfident. He recognized that he was indecisive, passive and without goals. He also reported that he had seen another psychologist the year before, at the insistence of one of his professors, but that he had not been helped at all, and he felt that he could do nothing about his problems.

He viewed his father as inadequate and *disgusting* and expressed his concern about being very like his father. He had great difficulty in saying that others would describe his mother and her family as domineering. However, he could not see this for himself. He felt that he was not aggressive, except in sports.

In the second interview, he was forced to concentrate on his family relationships. He could remember nothing before the age of thirteen. In this session, his repressed hostility toward his mother, and his subsequent feeling of guilt when he was much younger, surfaced. Although he currently did not want to disappoint his mother, he knew that his lack of goals hurt her very much.

The next session he reported that his mother had told him that his father had been in the Navy when Bert was two years old. During this period Bert had been with his mother and was placed in a day care center at age two and one-half. Until he entered elementary school, he was obstinate and irritable and then he became "very good." He clung to his mother, avoided other children and developed fear of people, the dark and dogs.

From the psychologist's view, Bert was typical of the child who was controlled, dependent and frightened. There were instances of rebelliousness on his part that were quickly repressed by him. He had been unable to develop a positive concept of self. He felt helpless and dependent. He demonstrated the negative aspects of Erikson's (1950) stages of development that occur in a restricted family milieu. Pathogenic factors were present in the family relationships.

Schema of Negative Job-Seeking Behavior

The dynamic process of negative job-seeking behavior related by Stevens (1962) and Stevens and Schneider (1967a) can be diagrammed as follows:

Needs → Fantasy Goals → Confusion → Unrealistic Job Goals

The process may be described as starting with the basic need of the individual for identity and recognition. This can produce fantasy goals which usually involve status and prestige-level jobs. However, in this instance, fantasy tends to become a means of expressing wish fulfillment that is untempered by reality considerations. Confused and vague goals and dependent, passive behavior evolve from the constricted family social environment. The individual tends not to develop a sense of identity or a strong concept of self and seems to be floundering.

The values and goals of the dominant parent tend to be taken over by the individual as his or her own. Because of the fear of disapproval from that parent, the individual has not developed a sense of his or her own abilities, interests and values, etc., that can affect a choice of career and job goals. In fact, data about career and job options tends not to be explored, collected and considered. Thus, the lack of action in exploration is an expression of passivity. The balancing of personal, internal factors with the realities of the labor market is not achieved without such information. Therefore, the narrowing of options and crystallization of job goals are not possible. Consequently, the job seeker's confusion continues concerning a career direction to pursue.

For the person with the negative job-seeking behavior pattern, the process is stunted, in that an active exploration for self-knowledge and for information about work options tends not to be engaged in. When a job goal that has been taken over from the dominant parent is expressed, it usually has not been explored and investigated. That job goal tends to be an unrealistic one for the job seeker. Increasingly, the job seeker's confusion about a job goal is frequently expressed in vague terms: "Get me a job in ... uh ... any job will do."

Interview Cues Identifying Negative Job-Seeking Behavior

Cues to the placement counselor are the expressed expectation of the job seeker that the interviewer decide what career field he or she should enter or what job to seek. This is illustrated by the following interviewee's comments that are too frequently expressed by an individual with the negative job-seeking behavior pattern.

Job Seeker: Get me a job.

Placement
Counselor: What kind of a job are you interested in?

Job Seeker: Anything will do. It doesn't matter.

Placement
Counselor: Do you have anything in mind?

Job Seeker: No ... just get me a job.

OR

Job Seeker: Uh ... I want an interesting job.

Placement
Counselor: What would be an interesting job to you?

Job Seeker: I don't know . . . you have all the job listings.
              You must know what jobs are interesting.
              Just tell me which ones.

The vagueness about job goals of these job seekers and their dependence on the counselor to make decisions for them are evident from these opening remarks in a placement service interview.

Another cue to recognizing this pattern of job-seeking behavior is the job seeker's failure to actively explore options in the world of work, as well as his or her abilities, interests, limitations, needs, values, etc. Sometimes, there seems to be a passive resistance to do so. Counselors often have the impression that the individual is so immobilized and passive that, if the counselor could bore a hole in the job-seeker's head and pour in all the information that would be necessary to make the vocational choice, it would be gratefully received.

Such a job seeker tends to give the impression of going around and around in circles of confusion, unable to consider and integrate any occupational information that may be offered by the placement counselor as a basic outline of jobs in a field of work under discussion.

For example:

Job Seeker: I'd like some work with children. What could I do?
              I'm starting my graduate program now.

Placement
Counselor: There are a number of options, such as teaching,
              elementary school counseling . . . vocational counseling
              in high school . . . psychiatric social work where your
              training would enable you to work with children in
              special agencies with that specific focus . . . school
              psychologist . . . and, of course, if you become a certi-
              fied social worker or a certified psychologist, a private
              practice with children is always possible.

A brief mini-description of focus of tasks was given by the placement counselor for each position mentioned, with discussion of some of the differences and similarities that existed in comparison with each other, concerning work with children.

Job Seeker: Yes . . . but I want to work with children. What can I do?

The placement counselor repeated the previous information, giving a few additional details, and asked the job-seeker's reaction to the different options outlined.

> Job Seeker: Tell me what I can do. I want to work with children.

It can be clearly recognized that this job seeker could neither assimilate the information presented, nor relate to it in personal terms, and she leaves the impression of being unable to break out of the kind of circular thinking that was revealed by the responses that she made.

Because these job seekers do not explore either for knowledge about self or about career options, there often is an unrealistic quality to their interview responses. This is illustrated by the following:

> Job Seeker: I'm taking psychology courses . . . and I want a job.
>
> Placement
> Counselor: Have you thought about what you would want?
>
> Job Seeker: Yeah . . . got any jobs for a children's therapist in a state hospital? I could start this June.
>
> Placement
> Counselor: Uh . . . as an aide?
>
> Job Seeker: No, as a therapist. I can be more effective with kids than those doctors can.

After a review of the educational and experience requirements for such a position, he replied:

> Job Seeker: Look, I'd be better than all those Ph.D.'s and M.D.'s with their training and experience. I can help kids better.
>
> Placement
> Counselor: These requirements are the reality of the job market. The employers will consider you only after you have the necessary background. . . . We do have an aide's. . . .
>
> Job Seeker: Ah . . . But what *is* reality?

It is evident from this exchange that the job seeker's goal, although expressed in specific terms, was an expression of wish fulfillment, a fantasy in which he could see himself in this prestigious profession being more effective in the treatment of disturbed children than his colleagues. No consideration of requirements was involved in his thinking. Even after the interviewer specifically mentioned the importance of meeting the requirements of the profession, he still clung to his short-range job goal. This was a job goal which might better have been reached by long-term career planning. However, he was incapable of doing this and clung to his fantasy.

When any interview responses are made that are similar to the job-seeker's responses reported above, the counselor should be alerted to test during the interview for indications of the underlying dynamics described in this chapter. If the cues are confirmed by the counselor's exploration, then a referral for personal counseling needs to be made before the person will be able to use the placement counselor's help effectively.

SUMMARY

Job seekers with the negative job-seeking behavior pattern have vague goals that may be unrealistic, and they exhibit passive, dependent behavior, which is a function of their submissiveness, sensitivity and high level of neuroticism. They do not succeed in getting jobs.

They tend to take on the goals of significant others or to seek out others to make vocational decisions for them.

Their perception of their early social environment produces a basic mistrust, self-doubt and feelings of guilt, inferiority and identity confusion. Their family environment is constricting and has pathogenic aspects so that their behavior tends to become maladaptive.

Chapter Five

TRANSITIONAL JOB-SEEKING BEHAVIOR

The transitional job-seeking behavior pattern is the style of individuals who have a modicum of success in procuring jobs. It is the pattern in which the job seekers exhibit characteristics of vagueness that are frequently combined with specificity regarding some aspects of their job goals. They also exhibit an independence in their behavior, which is combined with dependent aspects as well. They exhibit one characteristic that is unique to them: that is, they tend to actively explore their capabilities, interests and skills, as well as their vocational options in the labor market. Exploration is not as prevalent an activity in either the positive or negative job-seeking behavior pattern. This could be true for the former because they have already crystallized their goals and do not need to engage in further exploration, and true for the latter because they are too passive and dependent on others to make their own career decisions.

In the initial research on job-seeking behavior cited in Chapter Two, these particular characteristics were identified as moderate placement readiness, because the job seekers in this study group were eventually successful in getting a job, even though it took them a longer period of time than it did those who had been identified as having high placement readiness (positive job-seeking behavior). They also were clearly very much more successful in obtaining a job than those with the identified characteristics of low placement readiness (negative job-seeking behavior). Placement interviewers who interviewed these job seekers found it difficult to predict whether they were ready or unready to procure employment. Their difficulty arose because the mixture of characteristics exhibited were typical of both of the other two patterns.

Apparently, employers also responded to them in a similar fashion, because most of them were not hired at first, but they eventually were hired as they began to exhibit a greater degree of specificity of job goals and their behavior became increasingly self-actualized.

DYNAMICS

Schneider and Stevens (1971) found that the characteristics of dependence (submissiveness) and independence (dominance) were not as clear-cut in their manifestations for job seekers with transitional job-seeking behavior as they were for individuals with the positive and negative job-seeking behavior patterns. The mixture of behaviors that were identified as the characteristics of both the positive and negative job-seeking behavior patterns by placement interviews contributed to this result.

In addition to their interest in dependence and independence being exhibited in transitional job-seeking behavior, the researchers were also interested in the incidence of counter-dependence that may be exhibited, inasmuch as counter-dependence is a form of dependence that can appear to be an expression of independence and sometimes an exaggerated form of independence. They found that there were job seekers with counter-dependence in all three job-seeking behavior patterns, but that there was a higher incidence of it with individuals who exhibited the characteristics of either the positive or the transitional job-seeking behavior pattern than there was with individuals with the negative job-seeking behavior pattern.

Analogous in many aspects to the behavior of the counter-dependent individual who seeks assistance from a career counselor or a placement interviewer is Bordin's (1965) description of the counter-dependent patient as one who

> reacts to the help offered by the therapist as though it were excessive, inappropriate, debilitating or, in fact, unhelpful. He is likely to emphasize his ability to solve his own problems outside of therapy. He refers to others as oversolicitous and as interfering with him. This patient criticizes himself in terms of his inability to achieve. He speaks of the necessity of overcoming his deficiencies, mastering situations, taking himself in hand and controlling himself. He will often take an active, leading, even competitive role in therapy. He tries to achieve and retain control of the situation.

In the interview with the placement counselor, these counter-dependent job seekers will frequently inform the interviewer that his or her efforts are not helpful in getting them a job, and that they themselves can be more effective seeking work without the interviewer's assistance. Leading up to this point, their behavior has become increasingly challenging and obstinate in terms of the interviewer's suggestions. In many ways they seem to be like the old television ad for soap in which the young married woman declares: "Really mother! I'd rather do it myself!"

Some job seekers with transitional job-seeking behavior in the Schneider and Stevens (1971) study appeared to be assertive and even aggressive. They could impress an interviewer with their efforts to show insight and to push themselves forward. In many instances, they were considered to have the traits of job seekers with the positive job-seeking behavior pattern and were identified at first as having positive job-seeking behavior. However, any long contact with them usually revealed that their efforts were superficial. Actually, their aggressive actions expressed a personal denial of dependence.

Some of these counter-dependent individuals also seemed to exhibit contradictions in their behavior. During the interview they would seek job information, and yet, their attitude toward the job information that they sought was that it was of minor importance. There was a tendency for these individuals to discard information of any sort (be it job information or the results of vocational testing), despite the fact that they had requested the information. In actuality, little real insight into their behavior was demonstrated.

On the other hand, other job seekers with transitional job-seeking behavior were confused with job seekers who had negative job-seeking behavior, because of the passivity and dependence that they exhibited. It is frequently difficult to differentiate one from the other. However, there is one cue that can be used as a diagnostic tool, and that is the manner in which the individuals respond to occupational information. If the occupational information is not integrated into their thinking so that there is no movement toward weighing, considering, rejecting or accepting any given field of work as a possible tentative choice, then vagueness and confusion of job goals tend to persist. They are still in the negative job-seeking behavior pattern. They may seem to be literally going around and around in mental circles and do not seem to be making any progress toward narrowing the scope of their options to any given area of work.

However, when individuals show evidence of having assimilated information and of beginning to evaluate and assess it, then they are in the transitional job-seeking behavior pattern. It is this particular evaluation process that makes the difference. When individuals begin to involve themselves in an evaluation process, then they are in the transitional pattern of the job-seeking behavior and they do not remain in the negative pattern.

Effect of Family Environment

It is not surprising that Stevens and Schneider (1967b) found that these job seekers, who exhibit a mixture of the characteristics of both the positive and negative job-seeking behaviors, also have a mixture of the family and personal dynamics found with the individuals who have the positive or the negative pattern. Consequently, their typical family milieu incorporated some of the pathogenic circumstances found in the family environment of these individuals with the negative job-seeking behavior pattern which contributed to the development of inaccurate perceptions of their early social experiences (Stevens and Schneider, 1967b; Stevens, 1972, 1973, 1977).

Some of the healthier aspects found in the family milieu of individuals with the positive job-seeking behavior pattern also contributed to the development of accurate perceptions of their early social experiences.

One parent or the other, generally the father, was perceived to be successful. When a parent was not considered to be so, he or she usually was seen with understanding rather than with the seeming revulsion that was expressed about fathers by individuals with negative job-seeking behavior. Although sons seemed to be somewhat constricted, they nevertheless were capable of developing a relationship with their fathers so that their feelings of independence were not completely crushed.

Mothers tended to have high career goals for their children and tended to be overprotective, but they were less domineering than the mothers of those who had the negative job-seeking behavior pattern.

Because of the healthier emotional core and fewer pathogenic aspects in operation in this family milieu, job seekers with the transitional job-seeking behavior pattern are capable of mobilizing their personal resources to explore, to identify goals and to obtain jobs. They are not completely crushed. Although they are sometimes passive and dependent, they are also independent and are capable of the exploration that will enable them to find their career direction.

Development of the Self-Concept

There are indications from the interview responses of individuals with the transitional job-seeking behavior pattern that their self-concepts are neither as strong as the self-concepts of those individuals with the positive job-seeking behavior pattern, nor as poor as those of individuals with the negative behavior pattern. Considering the mixture of family dynamics and behaviors that exhibit characteristics of both the positive and negative job-seeking behavior patterns that are characteristic of individuals with transitional job-seeking behavior, this observation might be expected.

Metadimensions of the Self-Concepts

Super (1963) identified seven metadimensions of the self-concepts which are the trait characteristics people attribute to themselves. These are self-esteem, clarity, certainty, realism, abstraction, refinement and stability. Only four of Super's seven metadimensions of the self-concepts will be discussed in terms of their effect on the individual's transitional job-seeking behavior. The functions of self-esteem, clarity, certainty and realism are focused upon because their effect can be more readily observed in the interview behavior of job seekers with the transitional job-seeking behavior by the placement counselor than can that of the other metadimensions. These are empirical observations and have not been formally measured and tested. Nevertheless, they present a clue for future research on the effect all seven metadimensions may have on a jobseeker's ability to get a desired job when interviewed by an employer.

Self-Esteem. It is noted that many of those with the transitional jobseeking behavior pattern seem to present a modified picture profile of themselves. Frequently, their self-esteem seems not to be as high as that of job seekers with the positive job-seeking behavior pattern. Placement counselors or interviewers have noted that some job seekers with the transitional behavior pattern tend to modify their statements concerning their job qualifications for employment in a field of interest with qualifying adjectives which reflect their attitudes about themselves. This suggests that they do not have an awareness of the importance of their experience in meeting the qualifications of a job. Consequently, they do not give the interviewer the impression that they have the experience that either meets or closely relates to the requirements of the job that they seek.

They are seen by the employer not to be as viable candidates for a job as those with possibly weaker backgrounds, but who have presented their background in a more positive manner. Therefore, in so qualifying their attributes and experiences, they have raised some barriers that may prevent them from procuring a desired job.

Some typical examples follow. One job seeker said:

> "I *only* have had five years experience in accounting, and *just* two years of that has been in taxation, so I don't think I have much of a chance to get into the Internal Revenue Service."

Actually, this experience could be of interest to the IRS recruiter.

OR

Another candidate was seeking a personnel job in a large company. She was told that there was a new job vacancy reported to the placement office in a medium-sized company for an interviewer. The job required two years of interviewing experience in hiring personnel for middle-management jobs. She replied:

> "I've *only just* recruited candidates for clerical jobs and for office management in my current job. I *only* assisted the Management Recruiter once . . . maybe twice. . . . We hired the person whom I recommended."

Another job seeker, hoping to be hired as a designer upon hearing that there was an entry job opportunity with a designer who would train, replied:

> "I've done *some* designing, but I was *only* an apprentice."

Such devalued qualifications become self-defeating statements which may reinforce some aspects of the individuals' self-concepts that are based on distorted or misinterpreted perceptions of themselves that are based on their perceptions of earlier social experiences. Should these individuals have denied symbolization of their experiences to their social awareness, then their behavior would reflect this and would be consistent with their self-concepts. This is illustrated by the following statement made by a job applicant to the placement interviewer after his job interview with a corporate recruiter visiting the placement office:

> "When I was talking to that employer, he said that I kept putting down my own experience. I can't believe that I did such a thing!"

The tendency is for the individual not to accept the behavior which he or she has exhibited when such symbolizations are denied.

Clarity. Super (1963)[1] also indicated that, "Clarity may be related to

---

[1]From Super, Donald E.: *Career Development: Self Concept Theory* (New York: College Entrance Examination Board, 1963). Reprinted by permission. Copyright 1963 by the College Entrance Examination Board.

having a vocational preference, to the consistency of vocational preferences, [and] to ease of vocational decision making." Job seekers with the transitional job-seeking behavior pattern tend to be at different degrees of clarity in this sense. Many may have a preference for a field of work but have not clarified a desired job direction within a desired field. They reflect less clarity of self-concept in their responses than do those job seekers with positive job-seeking behavior. They may also be uncertain about the field in which they wish to work, and they tend to be exploring their work options by seeking information on what is available for them in terms of their background. Although unclear or vague about what they want to do, they are different from those with the negative job-seeking behavior pattern who request that the interviewer tell them what to do and give them a job. In contrast, these job seekers become involved in the process of exploration.

Examples of this follow. One woman said:

> "I want to do something in the communications field, but I'm really not sure just what . . . I've looked at publishing. I want to know more about other opportunities."

Another stated:

> "I'm wondering what I can do with a science major and my experience in writing and editing . . . if anything . . . that's what I want to discuss."

Certainty. The metadimension of certainty may also be reflected in the transitional job-seeking behavior pattern. This metadimension may not only be confused with the metadimension of clarity but also may be contaminated with general self-confidence. Nevertheless, its importance lies in the effect that a person's certainty of self has on the ability to make vocational decisions and to implement them.

It has been observed that job seekers who explore and identify their abilities, life skills, interests, needs, values and meaningful activity patterns with placement counselors tend to become increasingly certain of their attributes, so that they tend to be less vague in describing themselves to the interviewer or to the employer. It has also been noted by placement interviewers that when this occurs, these job seekers tend to receive job offers.

Realism. Realism, another metadimension of the self-concepts, according to Super (1963),[2] "denotes the degree of agreement between the individual's picture of himself and external, objective evidence of his status on the characteristics in question."

Again, it has been observed by placement counselors that those job seekers with the transitional job-seeking behavior pattern tend to exhibit more realism in this particular sense than those with the negative job-seeking behavior pattern. For example, an undergraduate inquired:

> "I'm a psych major . . . and I'd like to get some kind of experience to test the field for myself. . . . It could help me to choose my specialty for grad school. . . . Do you have any aide jobs that could give me some experience?"

This graduate exhibits more realism in his choice of job goal which is appropriate for him in terms of his background than did the undergraduate with negative job-seeking behavior who wished to have immediately a job as a child psychotherapist, as mentioned in Chapter Four.

Case Studies

An example of an individual who has the transitional job-seeking behavior pattern is Stacey, a college student who was in the second term of her junior year. She had not, as yet, declared her major, a choice the college administration expected her to have made no later than the beginning of the junior year.

She informed the counselor that she really knew exactly what she wanted to do. Most of her life she had helped out at home with a younger sister who was chronically ill with diabetes. She enjoyed doing this so much that she wanted to be a nurse. However, she did not do well in her science courses and had already found out from her inquiries that this would prevent her from being accepted into a nursing program.

When the counselor explored what her difficulty with science might have been, Stacey said she did not know. She repeated that she wanted to be a nurse, but she did not see how she could ever master the requisite subjects in science.

Using her basic interest as a springboard, the counselor suggested other helping career fields for her to explore. Stacey was interested in knowing the amount of science required for her involvement in social

---

[2]From Super, Donald E.: *Career Development: Self Concept Theory* (New York: College Entrance Examination Board, 1963). Reprinted by permission. Copyright 1963 by the College Entrance Examination Board.

work, counseling, health education, etc. She was willing to explore these suggestions but expressed concern that she might not have the background for them. She did not know what she had to offer.

Her feelings were recognized by the counselor, and Stacey said she wanted to know more about herself.

Stacey was introduced to Holland's Self-Directed Search (SDS) to determine her pattern of meaningful activities from the Holland typologies. This exercise helped her to identify fields of work that would bring her satisfaction. She also was given exercises to identify her values and skills developed from life's experiences. These gave her information about herself that she needed to use in assessing the career information that she would explore.

She had some difficulty in accepting the skills that emerged from her analysis of areas that turned out well for her, saying that her older sister and brother really achieved things. She wished that she could do things well. This was discussed with her in terms of her feelings and in terms of the items that she had selected from her personal experience.

She was introduced to the career literature, and another appointment was made to discuss her reactions to what she was exploring. When she returned for the discussion, she had covered only one area, and when the counselor raised questions, she read out loud from her notes each time. It felt to the counselor as though she was trying to control how the time in the interview was to be spent, as the reading of her notes cut the time for discussion. She finally summarized at the end of the appointment what aspects of the field appealed to her and on what areas she needed additional information. Apparently, an evaluation process was in operation. It was agreed that she would do further reading before making the next appointment.

Stacey was seen in the Career Library for several weeks after that. When the counselor asked her later how her exploration was going and if she would like to make an appointment to sort things out, she replied that she thought she could figure it out for herself, but that she would make an appointment if she needed help. She was observed in the Career Library a few times after that, but she did not make an appointment. Another time, the counselor expressed interest in her progress and she stated she was still working on it. She did not make another appointment.

Stacey demonstrates many behaviors that are typical of individuals with transitional job-seeking behavior. She was actually exploring, not only occupational information on careers related to her interest in helping people, but also her patterns and attributes to enhance her self-knowledge. There was also evidence from her discussion with the counselor on the first career field that she explored that she was evaluating and assessing this career information in terms of self-knowledge. She was also aware of what additional information she needed. She was engaged in some of the essential vocational tasks that lead to a crystallization of career choice.

She also exhibited independence in carrying through her occupational exploration in the Career Library. She was firm about being capable of making a career decision without further use of counseling. It suggests that she may have been masking feelings of dependence on the counselor in reaching a career decision about a choice of major by being independent in sorting out her reactions to the careers under study by herself. She had developed this decision-making skill as a result.

Another example of transitional job-seeking behavior is Carole, a senior with whom Stevens and Schneider (1967b) worked in their job-seeking behavior dynamics study.

She went to the placement counselor to explore both long-range and short-range vocational goals in view of her possible marriage during the summer. At first, she was confused about what she wanted to do but recognized that she was interested in people and was challenged by the variety of activities that she had performed in her part-time and summer jobs.

A variety of work tasks was a very important factor for her to consider in a job. She seemed unable to commit herself to a career choice. Although casual about it, it was evident that she had given a great deal of thought to it. She also had considered and identified her interests and values and recognized her abilities. An evaluation process was in operation. She expressed an interest in working in the field of communications and made arrangements with the counselor to review the career literature on publishing, advertising and public relations.

Carole returned to discuss the communications field with the counselor and to inquire about current salaries in these fields. In discussing these factors with the counselor, she crystallized a career choice. She asked for job leads in public relations, which were given.

As graduation neared, she did not return to the placement counselor. When she was contacted later, she reported that she had gone on her own job-hunting campaign, had accepted a job as a Girl Friday in a public relations firm and that she felt she had a good chance to learn the business. She was to start two weeks after her wedding.

Carole showed many indications that the developmental process of transitional job-seeking behavior was evolving into positive job-seeking behavior. Although she was at first confused about what she wanted to do, self-knowledge and knowledge of preferred work tasks enabled an evaluation process to operate while she explored career and job options.

She developed aspects of positive job-seeking behavior when she crystallized a job goal, exhibited self-actualized activity in a job hunt, and a job was procured.

Schema of Transitional Job-Seeking Behavior

The dynamic process of the transitional job-seeking behavior pattern can be diagrammed (Stevens, 1962; Stevens and Schneider, 1967a) as follows:

Needs → Fantasy Goals → Confusion → Exploration → Evaluation of External and Internal Factors

The process may be described as beginning with needs of the individual for identity and recognition, which may produce fantasy goals, and is followed by confusion about career direction. Because there are fewer pathogenic circumstances in this family environment than in the family milieu of those job seekers with the negative behavior pattern, there is a healthy aspect to the individual's personality from which self-actualized behavior can develop.

The tendency is toward active exploration of personal factors and career options, which is the key difference between individuals with the transitional pattern and those with the negative pattern who tend to remain passive. When an evaluation of job options is taken under consideration and these options are assessed in terms of inner personal factors, the range of these options is narrowed by this sorting-out process. Then the individual is on the way to crystallizing some tentative choices and specifying a desired job goal: that is, a repertoire of behaviors has developed that tends to lead in the direction of the positive job-seeking behavior pattern.

SUMMARY

Individuals exhibiting the characteristics of the transitional job-seeking behavior pattern have a mixture of the characteristics of both the positive and the negative job-seeking behavior patterns. They can be both crystallized and vague concerning aspects of their job goals, and they exhibit both self-actualization and independence as well as passivity and dependence in their job-seeking behavior.

Job seekers with transitional job-seeking behavior resemble those with the characteristics of the positive job-seeking behavior pattern more than they do those job seekers exhibiting the characteristics of the negative job-seeking behavior pattern. Undoubtedly, this explains why they succeeded in getting desired jobs, even though they do not obtain them as soon as do those job seekers with the characteristics of positive job-seeking behavior.

They present complex dynamics with which the placement counselor needs to work, and it is this group with whom the counseling trained placement interviewer can be most effective. In addition to aiding these individuals in the exploration of their work options and in the evaluation of the personal factors that need to be considered in choosing among their career options, the placement counselor can help them to develop an understanding of their behavior involved in solving their vocational problems.

The job seekers with transitional job-seeking behavior tend to respond to counseling interventions and move toward a solution, whereas the individuals with negative job-seeking behavior tend not to do so, depending on their passivity and core of mental health. An exception to this response to counseling is when job seekers are counter-dependent. Their tendency is to mask their feelings of dependence upon the counselor by attempting to display independence. These displays of independence can become exaggerated and may result in self-sabotage, if, by so doing, they do not allow themselves to obtain the help they seek.

Chapter Six

JOB–SEEKING BEHAVIOR
AND VOCATIONAL DEVELOPMENT

W hen job seekers first come to the placement service to obtain help
in finding a job, they may, in many instances, be seeking to
implement their self-concepts by finding appropriate positions. It is also
possible that they may be seeking jobs without being able to give them
definition and without having thought through their career directions.
The placement counselor or interviewer not only has to work with the
job-seekers' crystallization of vocational goals but also with the characteristics of their job-seeking behavior. Consequently, awareness of the relationship between the job-seekers' vocational development and their
behavior exhibited when seeking jobs can provide the framework for
understanding how to assist them in becoming increasingly effective in
their job-seeking efforts.

Certainly, the vocational development process theories of Ginzberg et
al. (1951) and Super et al. (1957) provide a theoretical base to be used by
the placement counselors as a diagnostic tool for identifying their clients'
stage of vocational development from their interview responses. It can
also be used to identify the pattern of their clients' job-seeking behavior.

An assessment that is based on theoretical constructs can suggest and
identify appropriate modes of assistance, as well as counseling strategies,
that the placement counselor may need to use. These are described in
Chapter Eight.

Job-seeking behavior will also be viewed from the theoretical developmental constructs of Holland (1959, 1966), LoCascio (1964) and Tiedeman
(1961).

VOCATIONAL DEVELOPMENT AND JOB–SEEKING BEHAVIOR

In the decade of the fifties, a spate of theories on vocational development emerged in the literature. In 1951, Ginzberg published the first

theory of vocational development that identified the stages through which a person makes an occupational choice in the formative years. This was followed by Super's (1957) theory that focused on the process of vocational development by means of identifying the developmental vocational tasks in a series of vocational life stages which had to be successfully completed before an individual could reach an ensuing stage of vocational development. In some aspects there are similarities between these two process theories, but one difference is that Super extended the vocational stages of development beyond Ginzberg's *Realistic Period*. These additional stages concern the individual's adjustment in the *Establishment, Maintenance* and *Decline Stages* in work.

Since both Ginzberg's and Super's theories describe the process that an individual goes through in order to make a vocational decision about career goals, job-seeking behavior patterns are first examined in view of these two theories of vocational development.

Ginzberg's Theory

Ginzberg (1951) defined a theory of occupational choice that described the process as continuous, irreversible and developmental:

> The process of occupational decision-making could be analyzed in terms of three periods—fantasy [Ages 6–11], tentative [Ages 11–18], and realistic choices [Ages 18 +]. These can be differentiated by the way in which the individual "translates" his impulses and needs into an occupational choice. In the fantasy period the youngster thinks about an occupation in terms of his wish to be an adult. He cannot assess his capacities or the opportunities and limitations of reality. He believes that he can be whatever he wants to be. His translations are arbitrary.

Individuals with the negative job-seeking behavior pattern verbalize vague goals that are frequently expressions of wish fulfillment untempered by reality considerations. Whereas Ginzberg's *Fantasy Period* covered the early period of childhood, in the placement office these job seekers ranged in age from the twenties through the early sixties. It was noted in the pilot study, which was conducted prior to the initial research on placement readiness, that such individuals were confused about what jobs they wanted. When they were able to identify a field of interest, they not only were unaware of the necessity to meet entry requirements for jobs, but they wished to have their fantasies immediately fulfilled without recognizing the role of personal factors and job requirements. In fact, they did not seem to know themselves very well. They were unable to identify important personal factors that they would need to know about themselves in order to make a realistic vocational decision. These job seekers were still in the Fantasy Period that should have been outgrown long ago.

It was evident that these individuals had not begun to explore for self-knowledge, nor had they explored the breadth of possible vocational options that were available for their consideration. The starting point of exploration is to ask questions in order to obtain information. These job seekers asked very few questions during their placement interview, which reflected their passivity. It was found in the pilot study that they asked the lowest percentage of questions compared to the other two groups of job seekers.

This characteristic behavior is consistent with Ginzberg's Fantasy Period. The critical question for counselors is what developmental lack would cause such stunted growth that adults remained in a stage that was outgrown by the average eleven or twelve year old.

Following the Fantasy Period is the *Tentative Period*. According to Ginzberg (1951):

> The tentative period is characterized by the individual's recognition of the problem of deciding on a future occupation. The solution must be sought in terms of probable future satisfactions rather than in terms of current satisfactions. During this period, however, the translation is still almost exclusively in terms of subjective factors: interests, capacities, and values. In fact, as most individuals reach the end of this period, they recognize that their approach has been too subjective. They, therefore, consider their choices tentative, for they realize that an effective resolution requires the incorporation of reality considerations and this will be possible only on the basis of additional experience.... The period of tentative choices was divided into the interest, capacity, value, and transition stages.

Job seekers with the transitional job-seeking behavior pattern give evidence of being in Ginzberg's Tentative Period. Actually, they may be in any one of the stages that make up the Tentative Period. Some job seekers indicate their job goal in terms of their interests without evidence of having given consideration to other attributes. Other job seekers consider their job goal in terms of their capacities and/or values. An awareness of reality factors, of personal needs and of labor market conditions begins to develop, and when this occurs, the job seeker has reached Ginzberg's *Transition Stage*.

Reality factors are increasingly considered by the individual. Ginzberg identifies this development as the *Realistic Period,* which is subdivided into the *Exploration, Crystallization,* and *Specification Stages.* During this period the exploration, crystallization and specification of a vocational choice evolves.

Regarding the exploration process, Ginzberg (1951) said:

> The young adult is striving to link his decision making to reality. This is in contrast to the preceding period when his preoccupation was largely with subjective elements. But . . . even though his behavior during the exploration stage is increasingly "reality-oriented," the individual now makes a final attempt to link his choice effectively with his basic interests and values.

It was noted in the pilot study that, as a group, these job seekers exhibited a characteristic that was unique to those with moderate placement readiness (transitional job-seeking behavior pattern). Compared to the other job seekers, they asked the most questions. They were actively seeking information about available job options, as well as seeking self-knowledge about their interests, values and other personal factors in relation to their vocational options. Their behavior is what would be expected of job seekers who are in Ginzberg's Exploration Stage of the Realistic Period of development. According to Ginzberg (1951):

> An essential characteristic of the next stage, crystallization, is the quality of acceptance, which stands in contrast to the confused or vague activity, almost hyperactivity, of the exploration stage. Most individuals have now committed themselves to a vocational objective, at least to the extent of being able to direct their efforts henceforth to further their choice, even though they remain uncertain about the details. Crystallization is the culmination of the entire process. The prior stages contributed to effecting the crystallization; the final stage contributes to refinement.

> The final stage in the realistic period is specification, which involves specialization and planning within the area of choice.

Job seekers with the positive job-seeking behavior pattern express job goals that are crystallized, specific and realistic. A field of work has been identified, and also within that field specific job goals have been identified. In terms of their interests, values and abilities, their job goals tend to be appropriate and realistic. These job seekers are in Ginzberg's Realistic Period.

The stages of vocational development that Ginzberg defined are observable in the placement interview, since they are reflected in the characteristics of the job-seeking behavior patterns (Stevens, 1973). The placement counselor must deal with the occupational choice of job seekers when helping them to find a job. Therefore, this theory has specific and practical implications for the job interviewer (see Fig. 5).

Super's Theory

Super's (1957) stages of development are defined as a continuous, orderly, patterned process that is generally irreversible. The patterning process involves the individual's coping behavior with vocational developmental tasks which are related to work. If these tasks are successfully completed, they lead to the individual's being able to cope effectively with other vocational tasks that follow in time. However, if the individual fails to achieve these developmental tasks at a given time, he or she will experience difficulty in successfully coping with the other developmental tasks that follow.

The first two of Super's five vocational life stages are concerned with the developmental process of making a choice. As Super (1957) states, they are as follows:

1. *Growth Stage* (Birth–14)
   Self-concept develops through identification with key figures in family and in school; needs and fantasy are dominant early in this stage; interest and capacity become more important in this stage with increasing social participation and reality testing. Substages of the growth stage are:
   FANTASY (4–10). Needs are dominant; role playing in fantasy is important.
   INTEREST (11–12). Likes are the major determinant of aspirations and activities.
   CAPACITY (13–14). Abilities are given more weight, and job requirements (including training) are considered.
2. *Exploration Stage* (Ages 15–24)
   Self-examination, role tryouts, and occupational exploration take place in school, leisure activities, and part-time work. Substages of the exploration stage are:
   TENTATIVE (15–17). Needs, interests, capacities, values, and opportunities are all considered. Tentative choices are made and tried out in fantasy, discussion, courses, work, etc.
   TRANSITION (Ages 18–21). Reality considerations are given

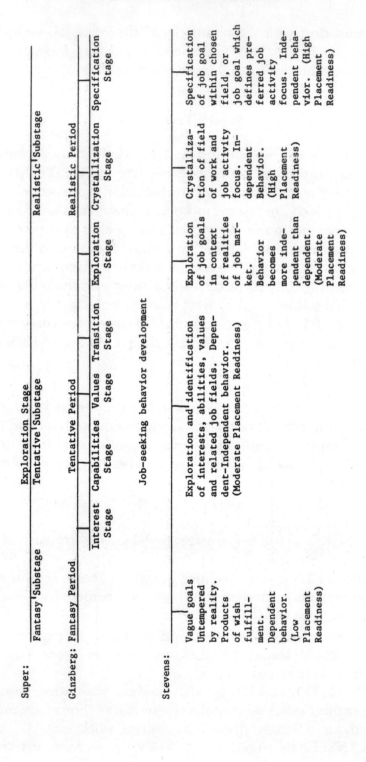

Figure 5. Relationship of Job-Seeking Behavior Development to Ginzberg's and Super's Theories of Vocational Development. From Nancy D. Stevens: Job-seeking behavior: A Segment of vocational development. *Journal of Vocational Behavior*, 3:209–219, 1973.

more weight as the youth enters labor market or professional training and attempts to implement a self-concept.

TRIAL (Ages 22–24). A seemingly appropriate field having been located, a beginning job in it is found and is tried out as a life work.

In terms of process, Super's stages of development are similar in scope and definition to Ginzberg's periods of vocational development, although his nomenclature differs slightly. His *Fantasy Substage* in the *Growth Stage* is comparable to Ginzberg's Fantasy Period. As noted, job seekers with the negative job-seeking behavior pattern would be in the Fantasy Substage (See Fig. 5). Super's *Interest* and *Capacity Substages* of the Growth Stage and his *Tentative Substage* of the Exploration Stage are also congruent with Ginzberg's Tentative Period. Job seekers with the transitional job-seeking behavior pattern who are considering their interests, capabilities and values are at this stage. Super's *Transition* and *Trial Substages* of the Exploration Stage with their components of increasing reality considerations and choice of appropriate field of work are comparable to Ginzberg's Realistic Period (See Fig. 5). Job seekers with the positive job-seeking behavior pattern are at this stage.

Super also enriches our understanding of the developmental process by his concept of vocational life tasks with which the individual must cope successfully in order to make a realistic choice that will implement his or her self-concept. He views the successful completion of these tasks at expected age periods to be the criterion for determining vocational maturity.

Super's (1957) other three stages deal with the vocational developmental tasks that the person must engage in after he or she has obtained a job. They are as follows:

3. *Establishment Stage* (Ages 25–44)

   Having found an appropriate field, effort is put forth to make a permanent place in it. There may be some trial early in this stage, with consequent shifting, but establishment may begin without trial, especially in the professions. Substages of the establishment stage are:

   TRIAL (Ages 25–30). The field of work presumed to be suitable may prove unsatisfactory, resulting in one or two changes before the life work is found or before it becomes clear that the life work will be a succession of unrelated jobs.

STABILIZATION (Ages 31–44). As the career pattern becomes clear, effort is put forth to stabilize, to make a secure place, in the world of work. For most persons these are the creative years.

4. *Maintenance Stage* (Ages 45–64)

Having made a place in the world of work, the concern is now to hold it. Little new ground is broken, but there is continuation along established lines.

5. *Decline Stage* (Ages 65 and over)

As physical and mental powers decline, work activity changes and in due course ceases. New roles must be developed; first that of selective participant and then that of observer rather than participant. Substages of this stage are:

DECELERATION (Ages 65–70). Sometimes at the time of official retirement, sometimes late in the maintenance stage, the pace of work slackens, duties are shifted, or the nature of the work is changed to suit declining capacities. Many men find part-time jobs to replace their full-time occupations.

RETIREMENT (Ages 71 and over). As with all the specified age limits, there are great variations from person to person. But, complete cessation of occupation comes for all in due course, to some easily and pleasantly, to others with difficulty and disappointment, and to some only with death.

It is noted at this point that unless a job seeker obtains a job, he or she will not be in a position to enter the *Establishment Stage*.

LoCascio's Theory

LoCascio's (1964) theory defines three units of vocational development. These are (1) continuous, (2) delayed and (3) impaired developmental units. When impaired vocational development is exhibited, it extends over a longer period of time than does delayed and continuous development. Continuous development extends over a shorter period of time than delayed development.

LoCascio identifies the behavior exhibited in each developmental unit. Individuals exhibiting the behavior of continuous development cope with a vocational task. "Vocationally relevant learning occurs during, and as a result of, coping with the vocational developmental task." Whereas, those who exhibit impaired development tend not to develop relevant vocational behavior as a result of experience. However, should some relevant learning occur, it is not incorporated into behavior. Consequently, relevant behavior is not brought to bear on the vocational task at hand.

Job seekers with the negative job-seeking behavior pattern exhibit impaired vocational development. Despite the fact that they seek help in finding a job from a placement counselor, they continue to be dependent on the interviewer to get them a job. They do not indicate in their behavior any learning relevant to the process of making a choice of job goal. In this regard, they seem to remain unaware of knowledge about themselves and about their career options. They are unaware of how to make appropriate career decisions, nor are they aware of how to organize a resume or how to handle themselves in an interview. They give evidence of not having successfully completed those developmental tasks that they were expected to have mastered in previous vocational life stages.

Job seekers who exhibit the transitional job-seeking behavior pattern tend to be in the process of working through the vocational tasks that need to have been accomplished before a realistic job goal can be crystallized. According to LoCascio's theory, these individuals would have delayed vocational development because they have not completed vocational tasks in the expected period of time. He sees this as resulting from their lack of awareness of the vocational developmental tasks that need to be performed and their unwillingness or inability to cope. However, they tend to have adequate behaviors with which to cope with such tasks because of the vocationally relevant learning from their vocational experiences. This results in their eventually coping with these tasks successfully enough, so that they are ready to cope with other vocational tasks that follow.

Job seekers with the transitional job-seeking behavior pattern *do succeed in obtaining jobs* in fields that they explore and crystallize as desired goals, when and as they successfully work through those developmental tasks that permit them to evolve the characteristics exhibited in positive job-seeking behavior; that is, exploration leading to crystallized fields of work, to specific job goals within these fields and to the development of self-actualized, positive goal-oriented behavior directed toward obtaining the job. They then obtain employment as these characteristics evolve, but it takes them a longer period of time than it does the job seekers with continuous vocational development who have already developed positive job-seeking behavior.

Job seekers with the characteristics of positive job-seeking behavior give evidence of having mastered the vocational tasks that they are expected to have accomplished in their early vocational life stages. They have crystallized and specified realistic job goals. They have had, according to LoCascio's theory, continuous vocational development in terms of their having learned vocationally relevant behaviors that they have obtained from vocational experiences.

Holland's Theory

Holland (1959) has defined a process of vocational choice through which an individual emerges with a vocational choice. In essence, it is a description of the process of a person exhibiting the characteristics of transitional job-seeking behavior and who is in the process of beginning to exhibit the characteristics of positive job-seeking behavior.

1. The person directs himself toward the major occupational class for which his development has impelled him by selecting the occupational class at the head of his particular hierarchy of classes. This dimension of choice is designated as the range of choice, or the variety of relatively different major choices.
2. Within a major class of occupations, the person's selection of an occupation is a function of his self-evaluation and his ability (intelligence) to perform adequately in his chosen environment.
3. Both of the above processes are mediated by a series of personal factors, including self-knowledge and evaluation, knowledge of occupational classes (range of information and the degree of differentiation between and within occupational environments), the orderliness of the developmental hierarchy; and a series of environmental factors including the range of potential environments, social pressures from family and peers, evaluations of employers and potential employers, and limitations—arbitrary in terms of the theory—imposed by socioeconomic resources and the physical environment.

Holland specifically focuses on the sociological influences that affect the individual who is making an occupational choice.

The above process that Holland defines is illustrated in the effect of the dynamics exhibited in job-seeking behavior. Job seekers with the transitional job-seeking behavior pattern are in the process of exploration in an effort to obtain self-knowledge and information about occupations. They are developing the foundation upon which to base their decisions regarding their choice of job goal within a field of work.

It is the job seekers with the positive behavior pattern who have acquired self-knowledge and knowledge about occupations in their fields of interest. They have assessed their occupational options in terms of their self-knowledge and have chosen job goals.

In contrast, job seekers with the negative behavior pattern do not make decisions about job goals independently. As a result of limitations arising from their perceptions that have evolved from their family environment, these job seekers have not developed accurate knowledge of self. They also are passive about acquiring information on different occupational fields and the jobs within them. Because of pressure from the dominant family members, they tend to take over the job goals of these significant others, rather than to choose a job goal based on evaluation of personal factors.

Holland (1966) has identified personality types by which the individuals perceive themselves as dependent or submissive (Conventional, Realistic, Social) and as independent (Artistic, Enterprising, Intellectual). An area for investigation is the relationship of the perceived dependence-independence of the six personality types to the three job-seeking behavior patterns: that is, do job seekers who are identified as being the Artistic or Enterprising or Investigative personality type tend to exhibit positive job-seeking behavior to a significant degree? Do the job seekers with the Conventional, Realistic or Social personality type tend to exhibit the negative job-seeking behavior pattern? Holland found independence to be a characteristic of the Artistic, Enterprising and Investigative types, and dependence a characteristic of the Conventional, Realistic and Social types.

Holland's theory is interesting, in that it not only defines the process of vocational choice, but it also defines the interrelationship between the individual's personality and the corresponding model work environment. A "near best fit" between the personality types and the occupations representing the related model environments has definite implications for career counseling. This is discussed in Chapter Eight.

Tiedeman's Theory

Tiedeman (1961) views vocational development as a decision-making process and identifies the structure that is entailed. His emphasis is on the compromise aspect of the vocational decision-making process.

He identifies two periods of decision making. The first is the *Period of Anticipation* which is subdivided into the following stages: (1) Exploration, (2) Crystallization, (3) Choice and (4) Specification.

In the *Exploration Stage*, opportunities are explored as are the alternative goals that are derived from the opportunities under consideration. This is the period when relevant factors are ordered and given meaning as they are perceived to relate to the goal. The individual attempts to measure himself or herself in relation to each option by considering capabilities, interest and occupational outlook. The social impact that these options may have upon the family is also taken into consideration.

During the *Crystallization Stage*, an organizing of relevant considerations related to each goal is in operation, so that, as Tiedeman (1961) states, "Sequences of tentative crystallizations, new explorations and recrystallizations can be part of this process."

Choice becomes imminent when crystallizations begin to stabilize. Tiedeman states that, "With choice, a particular goal, and its relevant field . . . orients the behavioral system of the person of relevance for his vocational development. This goal may be elected with varying degrees of certainty. . . . " The degree of the individual's rationality and emotionality, the complexity and the antagonism of the alternatives under consideration affect the decision.

Specification of "choice readies the individual to act upon his decision . . . (Tiedeman, 1961). The process of specification involves the lessening of self-doubts, the picturing of self in the occupation and the readying of the individual's action relevant to the realization of the chosen goal. It is this process that identifies the dynamic that is in operation when the person with the mixture of passive and self-actualized behaviors (transitional pattern) has identified a specific job goal and increasingly begins to exhibit movement toward an independent, self-actualized behavior (positive pattern). Tiedeman has identified the critical factor that stimulates the change from transitional job-seeking behavior to positive job-seeking behavior.

Tiedeman's second period of decision making is the *Period of Implementation and Adjustment*, which is concerned with the individual's adjustment to work and the implementation of his or her career. It consists of the following three stages: Induction, Transition and Maintenance.

During the *Stage of Induction*, the individual interacts with his or her social environment at work and eventually perceives acceptance. There is an assimilation of the individual's goal with the relevant purpose of the group.

The individual then enters the *Stage of Transition*. His or her behavior ceases to be responsive and becomes increasingly assertive. The group's goal and the individual's goal become modified if the individual is successful in working within the group.

The *Maintenance Stage* follows, and Tiedeman sees it as a "condition of dynamic equilibrium." Both the individual and the group strive to keep the structure that has evolved from their interaction. However, maintenance may become altered when there are changes within the group membership or when there are new strivings within the group which may change the status quo.

Both Super and Tiedeman have identified the process of adjustment to work after the job seeker has successfully obtained a job. What is the effect of the personality dynamics, which are exhibited in the characteristics of job-seeking behavior patterns, upon the career development of individuals within their work setting? Would employees with the characteristics of the positive job-seeking behavior pattern advance further and in a shorter period of time than would employees with the characteristics of the transitional job-seeking behavior pattern? This has not yet been explored and is an area for further research.

Vocational Maturity

Both Ginzberg (1951) and Super (1957) considered that an occupational choice is not made as an isolated event in time, but that it tends to be made at a developmental pace, in that any one stage of development is dependent upon the previous stage of development. Super (1972) indicates that it is the tasks which are inherent to each stage or substage within a vocational life stage that must be accomplished in order for the individual to be able to cope effectively with ensuing tasks in the evolving vocational life stages that follow.

When the individual accomplishes these tasks within the age span expected by society for them to be addressed and mastered, then the individual is developing vocational maturity. Initially, both Ginzberg and Super identified age ranges which are essentially similar for each of their developmental stages leading to an occupational choice. Ginzberg's Fantasy Period is between ages six to eleven; the Tentative Period encompasses the ages from eleven to eighteen and the Realistic Period from eighteen to twenty-four; and Super sets the age range for the Fantasy Substage of the Growth Stage from four to ten; the Interest Substage encompasses the ages of eleven to twelve and the Capacity Substage is from ages thirteen to fourteen. The Exploration Stage, which follows, consists of the Tentative Substage from ages fifteen to seventeen, the Transition Substage from ages eighteen to twenty-one, and the Trial Substage from ages twenty-two to twenty-four.

Ginzberg suggests that individuals who do not give evidence of conforming to the age ranges of the different stages may be considered as deviating from the pace of the process. This can be illustrated by the girl who knows at age five that she wishes to become an orthopedic surgeon because of her broken leg and never changes her ambition. Through life she makes the appropriate decisions and takes the appropriate actions that lead to her graduation from medical school years later. It can also be illustrated by the young adult in his or her thirties who is floundering because a career goal has not crystallized and uncertainty and vagueness about options still exist.

The age ranges that Ginzberg and Super have assigned to their developmental stages should not be considered as fixed but as general guidelines that enable the counselor to assess the pace of the job seekers' vocational development and consequently their vocational maturity and or immaturity.

However, it should be noted that these age ranges were identified in Ginzberg's and Super's research in the late forties and fifties. Since then, we have had the advent of television, so that space flight to the outer reaches of our planetary system, the Vietnam War, assassinations of our political and social leaders, terrorist activities, pictures of unemployment lines, closing factories and newly developed products are viewed in living rooms across the country. This has an effect on the pace of sophistication, awareness and development of people that could not have been anticipated when the first television set was run off the assembly line.

Osipow (1973) states that the process of career choice is also deeply imbedded in cultural and economic factors, so that an individual's development is affected by changing economic conditions and cultural influences during his or her lifetime. Therefore, intimacy with national events that the family television set provides could well be a factor that affects and changes the pace of vocational development.

Job seekers with negative job-seeking behavior, who in the early and later adult years state either vague job goals or express job goals that are manifestations of wish fulfillment untempered by reality considerations, are in the Fantasy Period of vocational development. According to Ginzberg's theory of occupational choice and Super's vocational life stages, fantasy role-playing for its own sake would generally occur during the early years of childhood to about age ten or eleven. However, these adults give no evidence during their placement interview of having assessed their interests, capabilities, values and various other reality considerations, which are tasks usually accomplished during adolescence through to the very early twenties. Consequently, their vocational development appears to be stunted. They have vocational immaturity.

Job seekers with the transitional job-seeking behavior pattern who are actively exploring opportunities available to them in the job market, as well as information regarding personal factors, are in the process of developing increased vocational maturity. If they are in their later adult years, they may be coping at a slower pace with those vocational tasks that are involved in choosing a vocational goal than are those who have already developed specific job goals. However, should they be in their early twenties, they would be coping with the vocational task of finding a job at a time when it would be expected of them to do so. These individuals, of course, would be coping at a faster pace of development than those job seekers who exhibit the characteristics of the negative job-seeking behavior pattern and who have fantasy goals that are an expression of wish fulfillment.

Consequently, those job seekers who exhibit the characteristics of the positive job-seeking behavior pattern, and who express specific job goals that have been arrived at through the assessment of reality factors, would have successfully completed the vocational tasks defined in Super's Growth and Exploration Stages and in Ginzberg's Tentative and Realistic Periods. As a result, they have reached the point where they have crystallized a field of work that they wish to pursue and are searching for a specific job that they desire. Having accomplished the developmental tasks that are expected of them, they have obtained vocational maturity.

Determining an occupational choice is an ongoing continuous process that may occur many times during an individual's work life. Many job seekers in their thirties, forties and fifties, etc., frequently seem to be seeking and exploring new opportunities and to be reassessing their evolving skills, interests, values, abilities and needs, which can lead to a change of job or even a change of career field. This would be the behavior expected of adults, and it represents the striving attempts of the self-actualized personality to reexamine and refine vocational options that are viable and which reflect an evolving self-concept of the job seeker. It also reflects an increasing vocational maturity.

However, if and when the job seekers' involvement in the exploration of personal factors in relation to viable job opportunities should be an *initial* exploration of such factors, then such adults may be considered as deviating from the expected behavior of individuals in their age group. Therefore, these job seekers would be exhibiting vocational immaturity. A careful assessment will have to be made of the job seeker by the counselor to determine the basis for their exploration, so that job seekers' vocational maturity can then be interpreted more accurately.

A Holistic Process Theory of Vocational Development

Five process theories have been reviewed in terms of the behavior exhibited in job-seeking behavior patterns. Ginzberg's (1951) theory deals with the developmental process of occupational choice. Super's (1957) theory views the process as a series of vocational life stages composed of developmental tasks that must be accomplished before the next stage can be entered by the individual. LoCascio (1964) views the process of vocational development as continuous, delayed, or impaired. Holland (1959) defines the process of exploration and the personal and sociological influences that affect that process. Tiedeman's (1961) theory regards vocational development as a decision-making process and gives understanding to the operational structure of exploration, crystallization, choice and specification of vocational goals.

Within the past thirty-five years, other theories of vocational development have also evolved. For example, Bordin, Nachmann and Segal (1963) considered occupational choice from a psychoanalytic perspective. Holland (1966) viewed vocational development as affected by personality which influences an orientation toward types of preferred work environments. Roe (1956) and Hoppock (1976) respectively considered the role of needs upon the development of a vocational choice.

Super (1957) described the tasks of the Trial Substage of the Exploration Stage as locating an appropriate field of work and *finding a job* in it which is carried out as a life's work. He does not consider the effect of the achievement or the lack of achievement in mastering these tasks upon the success or lack of success in getting that job.

Consequently, there is an important gap in vocational developmental theory, because it cannot be assumed that individuals will obtain a job that may be tried out as a life's work. Up to this point, most of the research and theory have been on aspects of vocational choice. There has been no attempt to combine the different theoretical aspects of vocational development and the operational dynamics of job-seeking behavior into a unified comprehensive process theory. Such a theory is needed in order to understand the full range of behaviors that are exhibited in making an occupational choice, as well as in obtaining the job that implements that choice. A comprehensive process theory can also provide counselors with a frame of reference with which to identify the job-seekers' stage of vocational development, their level of vocational maturity and the underlying dynamics that operate in their job-seeking behavior. It can also help to determine the type of counseling interventions that are appropriate for helping job seekers to understand how their personality dynamics affect their success in obtaining a job.

The following section offers postulates on the character and development of job-seeking behavior.

Postulates of Job Seeking Behavior

Five postulates are proposed:

1. In job-seeking behavior, the striving effort of an individual to obtain his or her chosen vocational goal is affected by the individual's perception of the need to work.

In the vocational situation, the individual's style of behavior is focused on his or her set goal, so that effort is expended in the direction of the goal. This includes the acquisition of training and skills to meet the requirements of the job, as well as the actual effort directed toward seeking appropriate jobs that are goal related.

Motivation to find a job is affected by the individual's realistic perception and evaluation of the need to work. The greater the perceived need to work, the greater amount of time and effort will the individual exert in finding employment. His or her job-seeking behavior will tend to become increasingly self-actualized.

Such a need may be an economic one: that is, a financial need to provide the basic necessities of life (food, clothing, and shelter for the family). The motivation may also be a psychological need for which it is essential to the individual to find creative self-expression, to develop a sense of belonging, or to have status or power. It may also be a social need to make friends. Motivation may also be based on the need to have the means to underwrite an activity, a hobby, or some item that will bring meaning and satisfaction to the person's life. The need to work may be caused by any one need or by a combination of needs that motivate the individual to seek a position. The perception of need to work can determine the force of his or her drive in seeking a job.

2. The perception of self affects the individual's job-seeking behavior.

The behavior exhibited in the individual's attempts to choose a career goal, to obtain the necessary qualifications for the desired goal, and to procure a desired job may either be positive or negative in its characteristics. Either type of behavior reflects the self-perception of the individual.

When an individual's self-perception is one of being unworthy of success and incapable of achieving it, then his or her job-seeking behavior in regard to obtaining a job goal tends to be negatively purposeful and seemingly self-defeating. Consequently, when these characteristics are exhibited in the interview behavior of an individual seeking a job, he or she is ineffective in obtaining a desired job.

On the other hand, when an individual's perception of self is one of being worthy and capable of achieving success, then his or her job-seeking behavior in regard to obtaining a job goal tends to be positively purposeful. When these characteristics are exhibited in the interview behavior of an individual seeking a job, he or she is effective in obtaining a desired job.

3. The level of development of an individual's vocational maturity affects his or her job-seeking behavior.

Super (1972) defines vocational maturity as "the behavior of the individual, compared with that of others coping with the same tasks." Therefore, when an adult has explored options and has identified job goals, he or she is giving evidence that the vocational tasks that we expect to be completed in previous life stages have been successfully accomplished. This is the effect of continuous vocational development that leads to vocational maturity. It is characteristic of job seekers with the positive job-seeking behavior pattern who succeed in procuring jobs.

However, when the development of an adult is observed to lag behind that of others who are of the same age range, in that job goals are unexplored and remain vague, then he or she would be evaluated as having vocational immaturity. This would be true of the individual with negative job-seeking behavior who has not successfully completed the vocational tasks expected and who, as a result, has impaired vocational development. This individual does not succeed in obtaining a job.

It would also be true of an adult with the transitional job-seeking behavior pattern who has delayed vocational development. Such an individual is in the process of coping with the vocational tasks of exploration and evaluation of career options which were expected to have been achieved in previous life stages. He or she may also exhibit vocational immaturity. However, this individual is engaged in the process of developing vocational maturity.

4. The individual's characteristic pattern of job-seeking behavior has a direct effect on his or her success in getting a job.

The job seeker who is successful in obtaining a job in a relatively short period of time has the positive job-seeking behavior pattern. He or she expresses specific and realistic job goals and exhibits self-actualized behavior in the search for a job. During the placement interview it is evident that career goals have been evaluated in terms of his or her skills, abilities, interests and values and that the trends in the labor market have been considered. Consequently, the job goals are realistically chosen. The job seeker with these characteristics also exhibits effective coping behavior. The behavior in seeking a job is characteristically positive, self-actualized and independent of outside direction. Success in obtaining a job occurs even in a very recessed labor market.

The job seeker who is unsuccessful in obtaining the job has the negative job-seeking behavior pattern. He or she appears to be confused because job goals are vaguely expressed. Interview responses indicate that skills, abilities, interests, values and possible options in the world of work are either unidentified or unevaluated. Goals tend to be based on fantasy and wish fulfillment rather than on reality considerations.

The job seeker's behavior in seeking a job is characteristically passive and dependent to the point of permitting, and frequently seeking, others to decide for him or her what job to apply for and to obtain it for him or her. Vocational behavior is passive and dependent and may be negatively purposeful and self-defeating in character. Success in getting a job, even in a very good labor market, rarely occurs.

The job seeker who does succeed in getting a job, but in a longer period of time than the job seeker with the positive-oriented job-seeking behavior pattern, has the transitional pattern.

A mixture of coping behaviors found to be characteristic of both the positive and negative job-seeking behavior patterns is exhibited. Dependence and passivity, as well as self-actualization and independence, are characteristic behaviors. Expressed job goals have components of crystallization and vagueness. Exploration to gather information about self and about career options, which are necessary for job goals to become clearly identified, defined and realistic, is actively engaged in as a primary vocational activity.

As a result, it is self-actualization that enables a person to reach out to explore career options as well as to obtain chosen job goals. It is when an individual's inclination to be passive conflicts with the inclination to be self-actualized that his or her ability to obtain jobs is impeded. This mixture of crucial behaviors lengthens the period of time needed to procure a job that is desired.

5. Job-seeking behavior is a developmental process.

In 1955, Beilin abstracted principles of the general developmental process that can be applied to vocational development theory. They have applications to job-seeking behavior. Behavioral movement tends to be from the general, dependent, self-oriented and isolated toward the specific, independent, social and integrated. His specific criteria for general development are the following: (1) continuous process, (2) irreversibility, (3) differentiable patterns, (4) developmental preeminence, (5) maturation, (6) differentiation and integration, (7) developmental pace, (8) movement from dependence to independence, (9) movement from egocentric to social behavior, and (10) interaction and interdependence.

Using Beilin's principles of general development, job-seeking behavior can be viewed as a developmental process based on the following criteria:

(1) The development of effective job-seeking behavior is a continuous process.

Effective job-seeking behavior is founded on the crystallization of specific job goals and on self-actualized behavior. It is a continuous process of development.

It begins with the person at an early age fantasizing about what he or she wants to be when grown up and trying out that role in fantasy and play. This is followed by recognizing the occupations that are related to the person's emerging interests, abilities and values. As reality factors increasingly are considered, career options are explored and evaluated in terms of their relationship to what is known about self, so that an appropriate career field becomes crystallized and a specific job goal is chosen on the basis of a "near best fit" between what the individual desires to do and what is possible to do. When the job goal is specified, the person's job-seeking behavior becomes increasingly self-actualized and effective.

Movement toward more effective job-seeking behavior was observed in the recorded interviews of a job applicant participating in the pilot study that identified the characteristics of placement readiness. The interviews of one job seeker that were recorded over a period of time identified the job seeker as initially having vague job goals and dependent, passive behavior. The second interview which was recorded a few months later revealed that she was beginning to actively explore job options in terms of her interests and skills. In a later interview it was evident that she had integrated job information into her thinking and was evaluating her options in terms of her self-knowledge. As a result, she had discarded some of the job possibilities. Her job goals were beginning to be more realistic and specific, and her behavior became less dependent and more self-actualized.

(2) Job-seeking behavior is differentiable into patterns.

Three job-seeking behavior patterns have been identified. Each has its own characteristic behavior that reflects the individual's personality characteristics and stage of vocational development.

Job seekers exhibiting negative job-seeking behavior have vague job goals and exhibit dependence and passivity in their efforts to find a job. Those exhibiting positive job-seeking behavior have specific job goals and exhibit independence and self-actualization.

Those with transitional job-seeking behavior have job goals that are vague in some aspects and crystallized in others, and they exhibit both dependence and independence, self-actualization and passivity. Exhibited exploratory behavior is a unique characteristic of this pattern.

(3) The quality of movement from vague job goals to specific job goals reflects the normal developmental process of increasing maturation and integration of self.

There is a tendency for growth and development to be in the direction of greater differentiation. In psychological terms, this is an expression of self-actualization.

At first, the number of career goals that may be considered is broad in scope. Consequently, the individual is vague about what job goal is desired from among many available options. With increasing age, the number of options is narrowed as they are explored and evaluated in terms of increasing self-knowledge. And, as a sense of self-identity evolves, the focus on reality factors continues to be taken into consideration, so that many career possibilities are discarded as a result. This leads to the crystallization of a desired career field or fields. The evaluation process continues to be in operation so that a specific job goal is finally identified.

Consequently, over a period of time the individual selects a job goal that implements his or her self-concept. Increasing vocational maturity is developed as the individual successfully completes the vocational tasks that are involved in this process from which a specific job goal evolves.

(4) The development of the characteristics of positive job-seeking behavior is an irreversible process.

For the integrated, mature and healthy individual, growth and development can only be in the direction toward greater differentiation, so that job-seeking behavior becomes less passive and dependent and more independent and self-actualized. Job goals also become less vague and increasingly crystallized and specific.

Movement can only occur in reverse from independent, self-actualized behavior and specific job goals to dependent, passive behavior and vague job goals should the individual's personality organization disintegrate.

(5) The evolution of effective job-seeking behavior occurs at a developmental pace.

For the individual with positive job-seeking behavior, the pace of development tends to be rapid at the start and slows down with time. That is to say, with the increasing age and maturity of the individual, the number of career options tends to decrease, especially after the exploration and evaluation of tentative choices.

For the individual with negative job-seeking behavior, the pace of development is stunted. With increasing age, the range of career options tends not to decrease. This is caused by the person's inner dynamics which inhibit him or her from obtaining self-knowledge and occupational information with which to evaluate career options. Therefore, the broad scope of vocational possibilities is not reduced in size. Confusion about what to pursue persists.

(6) As growth and development occur, there is a tendency for increasing independence to be exhibited in the individual's job-seeking behavior.

The healthy and maturing individual increasingly becomes less influenced by the preferences of others and more influenced by his or her own preferences. The person with the positive job-seeking behavior pattern crystallizes and specifies a choice by the process of evaluating the many factors affecting his or her choice. Whereas, the individual with the negative job-seeking behavior pattern whose development has been inhibited by the pathogenic circumstances in his or her family environment tends to be dependent on the preferences of others regarding the selection of a career goal.

(7) A job seeker will focus his or her energy on a given vocational task in a time frame of relevance.

This is the principle of developmental preeminence. In establishing the identity of a job goal, the individual concentrates on the vocational tasks in the different stages of vocational development. It involves focusing on the identification of his or her interests, abilities, values and reality factors that can affect career choices. Effort is concentrated on the exploration of potential career options and on their evaluation as viable career goals. As a result, job goals become specified in time.

In the job-seeking process the individual will focus on different aspects of the job search process, such as obtaining job leads and developing the necessary tools of the job search: the resume and interview skills. Much effort is expended on resume construction and interview skills development because they are essential aids for the job interview with the employer.

(8) The vocational tasks that need to be successfully completed for an effective job

search are dependent on the job seeker's achievement of previous vocational tasks in his or her earlier vocational life stages.

Interaction and interdependence are in operation. There can be either a simultaneous or a successive effect of the many vocational tasks that the individual has already accomplished upon the other vocational tasks that will follow. This would be true, for example, when the individual is preparing a resume for his or her job search. Resume construction is dependent on the previous tasks that led to crystallizing a job goal. The resume tends to be effective in obtaining a job interview with an employer when it focuses on a specific job goal and when appropriate personal data concerning abilities, skills and experience are related on the resume to that job goal.

On the other hand, when vocational tasks have not been achieved or have been delayed in their completion, the individuals' vocational behavior is affected by the many tasks that have not been accomplished. For example, they generally have difficulty in specifying job goals and, consequently, in constructing effective resumes which are contingent on definite goals. Because job seekers with indefinite goals tend not to get jobs, the job-seeking behavior of these individuals tends to be ineffective. When these tasks are completed through counseling interventions, then their job-seeking behavior will become more effective.

(9) Reality considerations increasingly affect job-seeking behavior.

As the vocationally maturing individual moves from negative or transitional job-seeking behavior to positive job-seeking behavior, his or her behavior is increasingly affected by reality considerations. When the individual's perceptions of experience are accurately perceived, reality considerations become prominent in the career choice process. They play an important role in determining what work the individual decides to seek. Because of personality factors and labor market conditions, a compromise frequently tends to be effected between what the individual wishes to do and what is possible to do in the world of work. Therefore, when these reality factors are considered, job goals become increasingly realistic and appropriate. This is exhibited by the job seekers with positive job-seeking behavior.

On the other hand, when experience is inaccurately perceived, vocational choices tend to be unrealistic and expressions of wish fulfillment. Inaccurate perceptions of the social environment appear to inhibit the process of reality factors becoming effectively recognized and considered in making a vocational choice. Consequently, job goals tend to be unrealistic and inappropriate. This is exhibited by the job seekers with negative job-seeking behavior.

A Holistic Developmental Process

The behaviors exhibited at the two ends of the vocational development continuum have been identified. Ginzberg (1951) and Super (1957) have established the developmental processes that are involved in making a vocational choice. Super (1957) and Tiedeman (1961) have identified the developmental processes of adjusting to work over a span of years.

Super's theory assumes that the individual chooses his or her field of work, finds a job in that field and tries the job out as a possible life's work. However, it has been demonstrated that a job does not necessarily follow after an occupational choice has been made. Job seekers who have impaired vocational development and whose job goals are determined by the preferences of others do not succeed in obtaining jobs, even when there is a shortage of workers in the labor market. It is, of course, the job seekers who have continuous vocational development and whose job goals have been self-determined who succeed in getting jobs, even when there is a recessed market.

Using the principles of general development, the author has identified job-seeking behavior to be a developmental process. Therefore, positive job-seeking behavior is the segment of vocational behavior that is the bridge between making a vocational choice and its expected outcome of working in a job related to that choice. Job-seeking behavior is the missing link of vocational behavior that enables us to have for the first time a holistic process theory of vocational development (Stevens, 1973).

SUMMARY

Job-seeking behavior is a developmental process. It meets the definitions of Beilin's principles of general development applied to the vocational area.

Effective job-seeking behavior is affected by the degree of successful completion of the vocational tasks that society expects an individual to cope with, and the accomplishment of which leads to the crystallization of a realistic vocational choice and identification of a job goal. The choice of job goal is the end product of a continuous vocational developmental process, as characterized by the positive job-seeking behavior pattern. The pattern reflects vocational maturity.

Effective job-seeking behavior is also the striving, self-actualized effort of the job seeker to obtain his or her desired job goal. This is characteristic of the individual with the positive job-seeking behavior pattern which leads to the successful procurement of employment, even in a recessed labor market.

Negative job-seeking behavior is affected by an impaired vocational developmental process. The vague, unrealistic, confused goals that are exhibited reflect arrested vocational development and vocational immaturity. Even when there is a shortage of workers, job seekers with this pattern tend not to obtain jobs.

The transitional job-seeking behavior pattern reflects delayed vocational development. Individuals with this pattern are coping with the vocationally developmental tasks of exploring, crystallizing and assessing their vocational options in preparation for their next task of crystallizing and specifying a job choice. They do obtain jobs but not as quickly as those with the positive job-seeking behavior pattern.

The positive job-seeking behavior pattern, which reflects continuous vocational development, is the bridge of behavior that enables a person who has made an occupational choice to find work and enter the Establishment and/or Maintenance Stage of vocational development. Positive job-seeking behavior is the vocational behavior that bridges occupational choice and adjustment to work in the job procured.

Chapter Seven

CONFLICT IN JOB-SEEKING BEHAVIOR

It was noted in Chapter One that not all individuals are positively motivated in work. Some individuals have attitudes about working that are negative and that reflect a different set of values, feelings and dynamics from those who are job focused and work oriented. The placement counselor frequently has the impression that these job seekers are attempting to avoid either making vocational decisions or having success in obtaining a job. This observation seems to be a contradiction in terms: a job seeker who tries not to obtain a job; a counselee seeking assistance in clarifying a career direction who resists the process of exploring and narrowing the scope of career options for the purpose of crystallizing and specifying possible job goals. This chapter considers some of the mechanisms and dynamics underlying this type of self-defeating behavior, inasmuch as theories of vocational development have not taken into consideration the motivation to avoid work.

Zytowski (1965) points out that theories of vocational development have been influenced by the middle-class work ethic and do not consider the attitudes toward work, values and behaviors of individuals in the lower and upper socioeconomic levels. He identifies as an example the concerns of hoboes as being able to find sufficient income for a day's survival. They do not have a long-term commitment to a career as do many individuals from the middle class.

Such concerns have often been observed by placement interviewers. Individuals who are unemployed or who are underemployed frequently express in their interviews with the placement counselors their need for a given weekly salary. These job seekers are not focusing upon the potential future that the job may have, nor are they concerned with the fact that the duties of the job may not be the type of work that they like to do. They seem to be exhibiting behavior that is illustrative of Maslow's needs hierarchy (Lipsman, 1967). Their need for food, clothing and shelter must be addressed first before the higher needs, like career concerns, are considered as an important focus in their lives. For many, this behavior is practical and realistic.

On the other hand, the adult behavior of those who are very wealthy tends to be neutral toward work, rather than negative or positive. The wealthy tend to move neither toward a career direction, nor to avoid a career. Their concerns and interests are apt to find an outlet in activities other than work.

Of course, there are some exceptions to the general tendency of the upper social class to be neutral toward a career. Outstanding examples come to mind. To mention only a few: the Emperor of Japan is recognized as a marine biologist, Mrs. Jacqueline Kennedy Onassis is a very successful editor in the publishing field, Corliss Lamont was a professor at Columbia University, Franklin Roosevelt was president of the United States, and Eleanor Roosevelt was a member of our United Nations delegation, David Rockefeller is a banker, Dorothy Schiff was the publisher of the *New York Post*, and Gloria Vanderbilt is a successful artist and designer.

However, Zytowski (1965) notes that when individuals who are wealthy do become involved with career counseling, they tend to meander in their career considerations and are not as motivated to crystallize a choice as are others who have middle-class values. It has also been observed in placement interviews that when such individuals are exploring job options they tend to do so in a leisurely manner, and they often do not bring their exploration to closure. They could be described as lacking motivation to explore their career options. This observation supports Zytowski's statement.

AVOIDANCE BEHAVIOR

Stevens (1977) found that avoidance in making career decisions and in seeking job opportunities is also exhibited by job seekers who have a middle-class background. They may well be motivated by the middle-class ethic, but they erect "blocks" that prevent them from choosing career goals and from obtaining job offers. In a very real sense, this type of behavior is self-defeating for those who seek employment. Consequently, their behavior seems to the interviewer to be contradictory and confused.

These are individuals who seem to be interested in having exploratory interviews with employers for which they make appointments so that they can be considered as potential employees. As job applicants, they are usually well qualified, in that they meet the requirements that the employers demand for their job vacancies. The expectation of placement interviewers is that the job applicants will succeed in obtaining job offers.

However, upon recontacting these job applicants, placement interviewers have learned that the job was not obtained. It is frequently discovered that some of these job seekers did not keep their interview appointments with employers, while others, who kept their appointments, failed to participate sufficiently in their interviews to interest the employer. Still others responded to the employers' questions in monosyllables or they exhibited little interest in the employers' vacancies during their interviews. It was also observed that a few who were offered the jobs that they sought became undecided about accepting them. Such contradictory behavior indicates that there is inner conflict being exhibited.

Theory of Conflict

Lewin's analysis of conflict and field theory (Travers, 1963)[1] provides a basis for understanding the mechanisms used by individuals who are in conflict as they operate in their job-seeking behavior. His field theory follows.

Lewin viewed the totality of personal experience as an inner psycho logical environment. He called this phenomenal field a *life space* in order to distinguish it from the physical space of a person. As there is movement in physical space, so is psychological movement possible in the life space.

The life space contains objects which consist of the person, his or her goals, perceptions, ideas, evaluations as well as the barriers which can restrict movement. How these objects are perceived in the person's inner psychological environment will determine the individual's physical and verbal behavior. Lewin considers behavior as a function which the individual structures, so that he or she can move toward objects or situations as well as away from them. When the individual moves toward situations, these objects have positive valences. When he or she moves away from situations, these objects have negative valences. When anxiety is per-

---

[1]Travers, Robert, M.W.: Perceptual phenomenological approaches to learning. In Travers: *Essentials of Learning: An Overview for Students of Education*, pp. 451–459. Copyright 1963 by Robert M. W. Travers. Reprinted with permission of Macmillan Publishing Company.

ceived in regard to objects or situations, they become repelling and individuals will try to avoid them.

Lewin's analysis of conflict is based on this valence concept. Conflict results whenever individuals perceive the need to move in more than one direction, even though to move in more than one direction is impossible. Anxiety results and tension increases. Consequently, individuals may vascillate between going in one direction or another in an attempt to reduce this tension.

Lewin's categories of conflict are approach-approach, approach-avoidance, avoidance-avoidance and leaving-the-field. Stevens (1977) identified the types of conflict that tend to be exhibited by individuals who exhibit the characteristics of each of the three job-seeking behavior patterns.

Approach-Approach Conflict

The job applicant with the characteristics of the positive job-seeking behavior pattern tends not to exhibit much conflict in his or her behavior. Conflict, when it occurs, may be exhibited when the job seeker has the prospect of more than one job offer to consider accepting. This situation would be typical of the approach-approach type of conflict that involves two or more positive valences.

When a job seeker has more than one job offer from which only one can be chosen, he or she actually may feel drawn toward each job. Each job possibility has a positive valence. At first, the tendency is the desire to accept each one of the job offers which are positive valences. However, this is not possible. In considering the job offers, one job will seem to be the most attractive. However, it can begin to lose some of its initial attraction and it recedes in primary focus. The prospect of another job offer is considered and it becomes increasingly attractive. One by one each job opportunity becomes the focus of attention as the attraction of other job offers continues to fluctuate. There is no discarding of job offers from consideration at this point, so that a choice cannot be made.

When the placement counselor is consulted, the job seeker can be helped to assess these job offers in terms of his or her abilities, interests, skills, needs, values, limitations, and long-range goals. As a result of this process, job offers usually can be evaluated and some offers are discarded. Therefore, it is possible for the individual to move toward accepting one of the job options. A job seeker who has the positive job-seeking behavior characteristics tends to resolve this conflict in a reasonable amount of time. Although a problem, it is not necessarily a serious problem.

However, should an individual give evidence of being unable to balance personal and reality factors that need to be considered in terms of his or her job offers, a sorting out of options is not possible. The person continues to be attracted to one opportunity and then to another without being able to resolve the conflict. This vascillating behavior does not lead to a vocational decision and is suggestive of a serious inner conflict that needs referral for personal counseling. Although this problem manifests itself in vocational behavior, the placement counselor does not necessarily have the training to help the client with the underlying dynamics that contribute to this type of behavior. A referral needs to be made to professionals who are trained to help clients with emotional problems.

Approach-Avoidance Conflict

The job seeker who exhibits the characteristics of transitional job-seeking behavior tends to exhibit the approach-avoidance model of conflict. Approach-avoidance conflict evolves when the job seeker perceives a job offer to have both positive and negative valences associated with it. The behavior that is associated with this type of conflict is vascillation between moving toward and moving away from the job goal. This would be characteristic of the job seeker who exhibits both self-actualization and passivity in job-seeking behavior.

This can occur when a job seeker applies for a job in which he or she is interested (positive valence) but, nevertheless, feels that there is an aspect of the job that is disliked (negative valence). There may be fear that there are some job responsibilities that cannot be performed successfully, or the duties may seem to be boring, or the employer may be disliked, the salary may be too low, or the geographic location too far from home, etc. These negative valences begin to operate during the interview, so that the job-seeker's interest decreases for the job for which he or she is applying. Consequently, when the employer indicates interest in the job applicant, he or she may decide not to pursue the suggestions concerning further steps that must be taken in preparation for a second or third interview (negative valence).

However, when the job seeker is at a psychological distance from the job interview, the negative valences begin to weaken. As a result, the positive valences begin to strengthen to the point where he or she may actually follow through with the employer's suggestions that were made for the purpose of further consideration for employment. Consequently, transcripts and references are sent to the employer as requested, and the employer may be contacted at the suggested time.

At the time of the second interview, the positive valences again begin to weaken and the negative valences strengthen, so that the job seeker is motivated to withdraw from the competition. Whereas a strong commitment of interest in the work might be what is needed to obtain the job offer, he or she leaves without confirming an interest. Following the interview, the negative valences again recede and the positive valences strengthen. Once again, the job seeker feels some interest in the job for which application has been made.

As long as the personality dynamics remain unchanged, inner conflict can occur whenever he or she participates again in job interviews. The behavioral responses to negative valences perceived in job opportunities will be repeated, so that the individual will continue to seesaw between applying for and withdrawing from job opportunities. This behavior strongly indicates that personal counseling is necessary in order for it to become modified and less self-defeating.

Avoidance-Avoidance Conflict

The job seeker who has the vague goals and passive, dependent behavior of the negative job-seeking behavior pattern tends to exhibit the avoidance-avoidance model of conflict. This type of conflict exists when the job seeker perceives two or more situations that he or she wishes to avoid (negative valences), when in actuality it is only possible to avoid one situation at a given moment in time.

The individual who is under heavy family pressure to achieve by obtaining a job considered by the family to be a good opportunity, could well wish to avoid having to take such a job (negative valence). This can be especially so if he or she is uncertain about career goals. The individual also feels compelled to apply for the job, because not to do so could result in additional unpleasantness from the domineering family member with the driving ambitions. Avoidance of this contingency (negative valence) is also desired. Therefore, the job seeker is in conflict.

When such a job seeker does go for an interview, behavior may express reluctance to apply for jobs that the significant other urged upon him or her. This may be exhibited by being late for appointments, responding to the employers' questions in monosyllabic phrases, describing experiences with negatively loaded phrases ("I have *only* two years experience" or "I *just* have a minor in economics"), or by making no attempt to indicate possession of related experience to the job responsibilities. Consequently, the employer is unable to form a positive impression of the applicant. Therefore, the employers' interest wanes and the job is not offered.

This behavior is self-defeating, and such behavior is a successful mechanism for not getting job offers. By keeping an appointment with the employer, it is hoped that family derision for not getting the job will be avoided. Therefore, it could be viewed that it is not the fault of the individual that he or she is still unemployed.

According to Lewin's theory, failing to get the job can only be a temporary release from the feelings of inner conflict. The cycle will begin again the next time there is family pressure to obtain employment in a setting or field that is desired by the significant other but in which the job seeker is not interested. This type of conflict is very serious in nature and cannot be resolved in the placement office. A referral for personal counseling is essential.

Leaving the Field

Another response to inner conflict can be expressed in job-seeking behavior in which the job seeker attempts to avoid the situation that provokes the conflict by escaping from it. This can occur when the negative valences that are perceived in the situation of applying for a job are so overwhelming that the anxiety level is increased to the point where the individual cannot function in the job-seeking process. A job seeker who is passive and dependent in his or her job-seeking behavior and who has vague and confused job goals (negative job-seeking behavior pattern) may also cope in this manner.

The job seeker leaving the field may leave home appropriately dressed for the interview but never arrives for the appointment. It is also possible that he or she may reach the outer door of an employer's office but chooses to immediately enter the elevator and return to the ground floor. In such a manner, the job seeker can succeed in escaping from the job interview.

Often, the job seeker can neither cope with the anxiety that is heightened by unemployment, nor with the family's driving ambitions for him or her. Therefore, no attempt is made to compete in the labor market for a job. An attempt to give the appearance of going on job interviews may be made, but the motivation is strong to avoid job-seeking activity. However, by leaving the field, the job seeker does not resolve the inner conflicts that are so overwhelming. It is as ineffective in resolving the tension from conflict as are the approach-approach, approach-avoidance, avoidance-avoidance behaviors.

The job seeker with the mixture of personality characteristics exhibited in the transitional job-seeking behavior pattern may also exhibit another style of leaving the field when attempting to avoid the inner conflict involved in trying to get a job. Such a job seeker often will accept a position for which he or she is overqualified, even when offered a position for which personal qualifications are commensurate. This can occur when the person has a poor self-concept and little confidence in his or her abilities and skills that are needed to do the job, or when the competition from others who are working for the employer is feared. Although a high level of anxiety is present concerning work performance (negative valence), there is also some anxiety about the need to be self-supporting. However, the individual with the transitional job-seeking behavior pattern has healthier aspects to his or her personality foundation than does the person with the negative job-seeking behavior pattern (see Chap. Five). Therefore, the job seeker tends not to avoid taking a job as a passive solution to ease the feeling of anxiety. A job is accepted, but, in an attempt to balance anxieties, the individual tends to take a job for which he or she is overqualified.

In actuality, leaving the field in this manner does not really resolve the problem. It may compound it. Such an employee frequently becomes dissatisfied with work which is unchallenging and loses self-respect for working in a job beneath his or her ability. Nor does the person hired to do such work respect or regard the employer highly. The need for counseling is again indicated.

To express it in Lewin's terms, as long as there are "objects" pertaining to job-seeking behavior in the individual's life space that are perceived as negative valences, the dynamics of conflict cannot change. Conflicts exhibited in job-seeking behavior seriously impair the job seeker's effectiveness in obtaining a job. For the job applicant, the reduction of perceived negative valences through personal counseling is necessary before behavior can be free from the effects of emotional conflict in the job-seeking process.

Fear of Success

There is some evidence that sex differences may play a role in avoidance behavior when the inner conflict involves successful achievement in occupational status. Initially, Horner's (1972) research studies on the motivation to avoid success found that many white women feared social rejection and experienced a sex-role conflict when they competed with men for achievement. Consequently, they tended to adjust their behavior by internalizing sex-role stereotypes to lessen their feelings of conflict.

Kripke (1980)[2] found that women's motivation to avoid success was associated with the expectations of their roles in life that their mothers had for them. Women with high motivation to avoid success associated with their mother's expectations that they be family minded. On the other hand, those with low motivation to avoid success focused on their inner-directedness and on the development of their potential as important goals for their lives.

Esposito (1977) found that women with high motivation to avoid success aspired to occupations that were typical of traditional sex-role stereotyped occupations. These included physical therapist, medical technologist, dental hygienist, nurse and elementary school teacher. On the other hand, women with low motivation to avoid success expressed interest in pioneer occupations for women, such as physician, lawyer, podiatrist, reporter and biologist. His findings are congruent with Horner's results.

Other studies by Alper (1973), Macdonald and Hyde (1980), Monahan, Kuhn and Shaver (1974), Schnitzer (1977) and Sherman (1982) supported Horner's findings regarding the motivation of women to avoid success. However, Depner and O'Leary (1976) and Peplau (1976) found that there was no relationship between fear of success and women's perception of their gender role.

Evidence from the literature has suggested that fear of success and subsequent motivation to avoid it may well be a phenomenon of white

---

[2]Kripke, Carol F.: The motive to avoid success and its impact on vocational choices of senior college women. *Dissertation Abstracts International, 41/05A:*2016–2017, 1980.

women. So far, there is some evidence that women with a different ethnic background seem not to exhibit this fear.

Samaniego's (1981)[3] study on the motivation of Hispanic American women found that motivation to avoid success was not found in her population of college juniors and seniors attending the senior colleges of The City University of New York.

Esposito (1977) found that Black women did not exhibit fear of success. However, he found that these college women chose occupations at lower educational levels than might otherwise have been expected. The occupations that they chose were in the fields of physical therapy, X-ray technology, dental hygiene and data processing. The majority of these women were of lower socioeconomic status, and Esposito feels that these women viewed college as the means of attaining well-paid and easily obtained positions because of the opportunities in the labor market. These chosen occupations met their need for being in an improved financial situation.

Fleming's (1978) study on black college women contradicts Esposito's findings. Her findings indicate that the performance of working-class black women did give evidence of becoming motivated to avoid success when in competition with males. It was also found that fear of success, along with the need for achievement, had a strong influence on their occupational aspirations. Approach-avoidance conflict affected their choice of majors, as well as their career goals, and especially any plans for entering the male-dominated professional careers in business, law and medicine. They feared that they would be viewed as aggressive should they become successful in a profession dominated by males.

On the other hand, she found that middle-class black women were not motivated to avoid success when in competition with males. Their mean level of fear of success actually decreased during competition with men, indicating that the test situation was nonthreatening for them. In this respect Fleming found that they seemed to be similar to white men.

Several research studies on the motivation of white males to avoid success, conducted by Feather and Raphelson (1974), Feather and Simon (1973), and Hoffman (1974), demonstrated either that men showed an

---

[3]Samaniego, Sandra: The motive to avoid academic and vocational success in Hispanic American women. *Dissertation Abstracts International, 41/08B:*3197, 1981.

"The dissertation titles and abstracts contained here are published with permission of University Microfilms International, publishers of *Dissertation Abstracts International* (copyright 1981 by University Microfilms International) and may not be reproduced without their prior permission."

increase in their fear of success or that the results were inconclusive. However, research on the avoidance of success in men and women, conducted by Argote, Fisher, McDonald and O'Neal (1976), Brown, Jennings and Vanik (1974), Morgan and Mausner (1973), all found that Horner's motivation to avoid success was experienced by men. Esposito (1977), however, found that fear of success in white men was related to high levels of educational aspiration in occupations. On the other hand, Levine and Crumrine (1975) found no significant differences between men and women in terms of fear of success. These research findings do not give a clear-cut picture.

Most research since the mid-seventies reflects an increase in the fear of success on the part of men, as well as a lessening of the fear for women. This may well be due to the positive acceptance of the women's liberation movement which has redefined women's sex roles and broadened the scope of acceptable behavior and achievement for women as is suggested by Feather and Simon (1973) and Morgan and Mausner (1973). Feather and Simon (1973) also suggest that for men the stress of competition may be affecting the attainment of occupational goals, because men increasingly are aware of the negative implications of competition for success.

Certainly, career and placement counselors have experienced a change in their clients during the past decade. Many men express freely their desire to make a mid-career change from a position of achievement to a job that will give them a more meaningful and less stressful experience. It is sometimes expressed by them that the women's liberation movement has also given them the freedom to change careers, because they have seen their wives happily enter fields previously denied to them. These men, consequently, do not feel trapped in a stressful job because they are the lone breadwinner.

Placement interviewers and counselors have often interviewed women who seemed to have the potential for jobs at a higher level of responsibility in business than those they sought. Frequently, their skills and background were considered to be outstanding qualifications for such jobs, and, yet, they expressed little interest in these jobs that were appropriate for their background. Most often, they would focus on the field of education or social service which are seen as typical occupational areas for women rather than on business where they would meet heavy competition from men.

Placement interviewers also need to be aware of the possibility that an occupation or job that pays well, but that may seem to be below the job-seeker's potential, may represent an opportunity for needed improvement in the financial situation of that individual. The interviewer needs to determine that the job-seeker's pursuit of such a job is not an attempt at leaving the field because of feelings of inadequacy to perform well.

Counselors also need to be aware of the possibility of the fear and anxiety that some women may feel regarding their femininity in relation to their vocational or professional options. On the other hand, an increasing number of women have combined positions of responsibility with the concerns of raising their families. Counselors can be helpful when they are aware of the stressful factors that can produce inner conflict as a result of the dual life that many women live as career women and wife and mother.

Fear of success may be based on neurotic conflict as well as on cultural stereotypes. Shaver (1976) notes that the patients of clinicians frequently exhibit "anxiety stemming from childhood conflicts with parents or siblings who threatened to retaliate when the patient excelled or asserted himself/herself." Powerful family emotional forces that strike the individual early in life, when he or she is most vulnerable, tend to continue to affect the individual on an unconscious level. Fear of family retaliation can develop a neurotic anxiety that is manifested as a fear of success.

The emotional forces exhibited in the family dynamics identified by Shaver have also been found by Stevens and Schneider (1967a&b) in the family dynamics of job seekers with the negative job-seeking behavior pattern, as well as in some aspects of the background of job seekers with the transitional job-seeking pattern. Undoubtedly, the dynamics that Shaver describes are also a factor in the conflict that is exhibited in job-seeking behavior.

A defense mechanism for coping with neurotic anxiety and fear of success is the self-defeating behavior that job seekers exhibit by means of avoidant behavior. When this behavior is recognized by the interviewer, the dynamics of fear and anxiety may be in operation. Need for personal counseling is indicated.

Fear of Failure

Fear of failure is an internal barrier that also affects vocational behavior and it can inhibit the effectiveness of job-seeking behavior. In the placement interview, the counselor can also see job seekers with avoidant behavior that is triggered by fear of failure. This self-defensive behavior is exhibited in fear of failure just as it is in the fear of success.

Shaver (1976) and Sadd, Lenauer, Shaver and Dunivant (1978) conclude that many measures of fear of success are similar to measures of fear of failure. Jackaway and Teevan (1976) point out that the definitions of the motives for Horner's (1972) fear of success scale and Birney's (1969) fear of failure scale are similar. Consequently, fear of success and fear of failure have not been clearly distinguished from each other but would appear to be closely related as avoidant responses to anxiety over achievement, although not necessarily on a continuum basis.

Some research studies have indicated that fear of failure is at least one factor that does have an effect on an individual's vocational behavior in terms of his or her career development, reality of vocational choice and vocational maturity.

Mahone's (1960) research examined the relationship of debilitating anxiety (fear of failure) to interests, ability and to the unreality of vocational choice. The expectation was confirmed that individuals with fear of failure would choose unrealistic occupations because they lacked information about their ability and the ability that was required for the field of their interest. It is, therefore, not surprising that he also found that individuals who had a high fear of failure and a low need for achievement were less accurate in estimating their own ability than were those who had a high need for achievement and a low level of fear of failure.

Mahone tested the level of aspiration of individuals who had a fear of failure. He used Atkinson's "theoretical model [1958] for predicting [the] level of aspiration from the relative strengths of [their] fear of failure and [their] need for achievement." Mahone states:

> He [Atkinson] has suggested that for persons with higher positive than negative achievement motive, the aroused motivation to approach success is at a maximum when the achievement task is of intermediate difficulty. For persons with relatively high negative achievement motive (i.e., fear of failure), the aroused motivation to avoid failure is also at a maximum when the task is of intermediate difficulty. If both a person's tendency to approach success and his tendency to avoid failure are simultaneously aroused, as they are in competitive achievement situations, his behavior when confronted by a task of intermediate difficulty clearly depends upon which motive is stronger.

Therefore, Mahone concludes that "the fearful person (more strongly motivated to avoid failure than to achieve success) should tend either to overaspire or to underaspire (i.e., to avoid the intermediate range of the risk continuum)."

Mahone found that subjects in his study with fear of failure were unrealistic in their choice of career goal in that they were either overaspiring or were underaspiring. In terms of overaspiration, fear of failure (debilitating anxiety) was a significantly related factor, whereas need for achievement was not. However, need for achievement was significantly related to the reality of the interest pattern, whereas fear of failure was not.

Saltoun (1980) found that fear of failure adversely affected vocational maturity, as well as the process of career planning, of the college white male students whom she studied. She found that they had a reluctance to gather both general information on their abilities and pertinent vocational information. They tended to avoid such tasks that would accomplish this end. Consequently, the process of their vocational exploration was impeded. They also devaluated the importance of vocational planning.

It is not surprising that she found that students with high levels of fear of failure were less vocationally mature than were students with low levels of fear of failure. The vocational maturity variables that were involved are CDI planning, CDI information, specificity of major, certainty of major, and satisfaction with occupation.

The results of Mahone's and Saltoun's studies have definite implications for job-seeking behavior. They offer insight into the passive behavior exhibited by individuals with the negative job-seeking behavior pattern, as well as into some aspects of the behavior of individuals with the transitional pattern.

A unique characteristic of many individuals with the transitional job-seeking behavior pattern is their exploration activity for self-knowledge and information about viable career options. However, others more closely resemble persons with negative job-seeking behavior, in that they seem to be passive and resistant to pursuing either self-knowledge or occupational information in depth. Although they occasionally seem willing to involve themselves in what may appear to be some of the easier tasks of exploring information, they fail to follow through in this activity for any length of time. This type of behavior suggests the behavior that Saltoun identified as an effect of fear of failure.

Fear of failure may account for some of their exhibited passivity, for, should these job seekers with negative job-seeking behavior characteristics exhibited in their behavior not succeed, they would tend to perceive themselves to be as hopeless a failure as their fathers. They would fear that their mothers would also regard them to be so. They avoid these risks by remaining passive.

Due to the lack of obtained occupational and self-knowledge, fear of failure can also be a factor in the unreality of the individuals' job goals as well as in their vocational immaturity. This is an area for further research in regard to job-seeking behavior.

Indecision and Indecisiveness

Frequently, job seekers appear to be in conflict about their career choices and job goals. They have not made a decision and seem to have difficulty in doing so.

Indecision

According to the Ginzberg (1951) and Super (1957) developmental theories of vocational choice, an individual's indecision regarding his or her vocational choice is caused by failure to have successfully evolved through the vocational stages of development at the expected age ranges. In many instances this uncompleted stage of development may be due to factors inhibiting the task of exploring self in relation to interests and abilities and vocational opportunities. When this is so, the individual does not have sufficient information to make a realistic decision with any degree of confidence. Consequently, he or she is undecided. Another reason may be that the individual will not make vocational decisions until there is a reason to do so, so that his or her decisions are delayed when compared to others in the same age group who have already crystallized or specified a vocational choice.

According to Salomone (1982), other reasons for indecision can be that persons with ability and talent have many alternative options that are open to them for consideration and that their interests may shift as a result of new experiences. This may be especially so for those who are responding to the positive reinforcements from significant others. Lack of information about occupations and their economic practicality, as well as a lack of information about decision-making skills, can contribute to indecision by causing a delay in making decisions.

Identification of Undecidedness

Holland and Holland (1977) identified three classifications of indecision. The first group contains those who delay making a decision because it does not seem important for them to do so at a given moment in time. This group, he feels, may include about 50 percent of the undecideds. Individuals in the second group have "a slight to moderate dose of immaturity, interpersonal incompetency, anxiety, and alienation. Perhaps they comprise a quarter of the undecideds. Finally, another quarter of the undecideds (third group) may have moderate to severe cases of immaturity, incompetency, anxiety, and alienation."

The Holland and Holland (1977) research identified "attitudes and skills: interpersonal incompetency, lack of self-confidence, lack of involvement, anxiety, an unclear and shifting identity, and poor decision-making skills" as characteristic of students who were undecided.

There are other characteristics related significantly to indecisiveness and indecision. Research by Galinsky and Fast (1966), Harren (1979), Hartman and Fuqua (1983), Holland, Gottfredson and Nafziger (1975), Holland and Holland (1977), Kelso (1975) and Munley (1977) have found that a lack of identity is an important factor. High levels of anxiety have also been identified by the research studies of Hawkins, Bradley and White (1977), Holland and Holland (1977), Kimes and Troth (1974), Mendonca and Siess (1976), Walsh and Lewis (1972) as being a factor that is in operation with vocationally undecided and indecisive subjects.

Locus of Control

Locus of control is another factor that seems to contribute to the difficulties of the undecided in choosing a vocational direction. Internal locus of control refers to the individual's perceived focus that he or she is responsible for the actions to be taken in response to negative and positive situations that arise in life. External locus of control places the perceived responsibility for negative and positive situations as being outside the individual's personal control and unrelated to his or her behavior. Cellini (1979), Hartman, Fuqua and Hartman (1983), and Kazin (1977) have found that undecided individuals have external locus of control.

Dependence

Dependence emerges as another factor. Ashby, Wall and Osipow (1966), and Cooper, Fuqua and Hartman (1984) found this to be a factor in their studies. Holland and Holland (1977), who found anomy to also be a factor, report that the McClosky and Schaar Anomy Scale (1965), which they used in their research, has a moderate-positive relationship with passivity.

Avoidance Mechanisms of the Undecided

Rosenberg (1977) reports that in his career counseling case load, "It is not unusual to see repeating behavior patterns of individuals trying not to make a career decision. The behavior patterns generally are learned and reinforced socially by parents, friends, teachers and counselors. . . ." He views these self-defeating coping behaviors as games dynamics.

The games that he describes are as follows:

(1) "Look How Hard I've Tried." Counselees give supportive evidence in terms of the number of times vocational tests have been taken, the length of time spent in trying to make a decision and the breadth of courses taken to find a field of choice.

Motivating factors to play this game are the "alleviation of guilt associated with not having made a career decision . . . [and] the desire to avoid responsibility for the decision." Their preference is to place the responsibility of a decision on the results of tests or on the advice of others.

(2) "If I Only Knew." These game players wait for an inspiration on what to do, rather than explore their personal interests, abilities, skills, etc. They are motivated by the fear of making the wrong decision. They feel that it is safer to make no decision at all.

(3) "Where The Jobs Are." Individuals who play this game lean toward jobs that are plentiful and seek information that may confirm what they have read or heard about. Often, they do not have the ability for these jobs, because aptitudes and interests have not been taken into consideration. Their primary motivation to choose well-paying job goals is often either from a need to earn money or from the pressure of significant others.

(4) "Time Crunch." These counselees never spend much time making a career decision. At the last moment they seek help the day prior, or on

the day, that such a decision is needed: for instance, registration for courses or declaring a major.

Rosenberg states that: "The primary motive of people who play this game is avoidance. They avoid looking at themselves, afraid of what they will see. Negative self-images are often found with these clients. Repressed anger is sometimes present."

(5) "Career Hide-and-Seek" or "Test and Tell." Persons who play this game purposely "withhold relevant personal information" that needs to be considered in a career decision. They may either say very little or present "irrelevant information and feelings." They are motivated to play this game because of fear of rejection. They seek a job that will propel them rather than begin thinking about and planning their career direction.

(6) "Yes, But." In this game, individuals block all counselor suggestions by "yes, but. . . . " As a result, alternatives are rejected and are unconsidered. By defeating the counselor's suggestions in this manner, these individuals protect themselves from the anxiety that would develop as a result of pursuing proposed career directions. The "yes, but" game also helps them to feel mentally superior to the counselor by dealing with his or her suggestions in this manner.

(7) "Leap, then Look." Individuals play this game in an effort to find the perfect job without exploring and analyzing their options. Consequently, they leave the job when they become disillusioned by the reality of the work. Actually, it is possible that they can change occupations many times in the course of a year. Because they fear that they might not like a job, they are motivated to avoid the reality obtained from exploring occupational information and working conditions. They also avoid looking at themselves, so that they neither know their capabilities, skills, etc., nor the relationship of their personal attributes to occupations.

(8) "Magic Occupation." Persons playing this game seek an occupation that will not only be perfect but will also "help them [to] become self-actualizing." They are afraid to deal with reality, and they seek an ideal environment devoid of friction. When they discover that the fantasized environment of a given occupation is not what they expected, they seek another environment.

(9) "Trapped." Persons in this game tend to be nonverbal and they reject occupations because of "their fear of being trapped" in them. Therefore, they avoid making career decisions in order to escape from becoming trapped. An approach-avoidance conflict can develop when they need to

find an occupation that will provide security and structure. They also have a need to avoid making a choice.

The above games are avoidance mechanisms that frequently are observed in interviews with job seekers who choose to remain vocationally undecided. Rosenberg's identification of these defensive strategies can assist placement counselors to recognize the dynamics operating in the placement interview.

Identification of Indecisiveness

Holland and Holland (1977) point out that when undecided students are not helped by the vocational counseling process involving workshops, testing, occupational information and counseling sessions, they may have an "indecisive disposition."

Salomone (1982) offers some behavioral guidelines from his observations that also help to identify the indecisive person. They are as follows:

1. Cannot or will not make a decision, even after a long, step-by-step, decision-making series of interviews;
2. Much repetition of the problem (almost wallowing in it) and many digressions to tangential issues;
3. High levels of ambivalence, resentment and frustration concerning their personal vocational situation;
4. Wants someone with a different perspective to provide answers—but will demean or ignore such answers. (This is speculation—answers were not given in counseling sessions.);
5. Is very dependent on another person (parent or parent type) for a clear sense of identity. Apparently, does not have a clear sense of separate identity;
6. Is very dependent emotionally and financially and probably wants to remain dependent but sees the future reality of independent existence and is frightened by it;
7. Is very manipulative; has a tendency to whine. Is immature on so many dimensions;
8. Motivation to change patterns of behavior is not very strong;
9. Not much self-confidence or self-esteem;
10. Tends to have an external locus of control—life controls this person;
11. Tendency to blame others for current dissatisfactory situation;

12. Has probably learned to be helpless and received much nurturance because of helpless-type behaviors.

Basically, these persons are struggling with the psychological benefits of dependency versus the possibility that independence (frightening as it is) may be better.

Van Matre and Cooper (1984) have presented a clinical classification scheme that diagnoses the level of the decided-undecided state and the decisiveness-indecisiveness trait. These are "two primary dimensions or continua along which delays or dysfunctions may occur in career decision making." The state of decidedness-undecidedness refers to the transitory level of indecision, and the decisiveness-indecisiveness trait refers to an enduring tendency that is consistent in any decision-making task.

Using their diagnostic scheme, it is possible to determine the degree of decision or indecision in relation to decisiveness and indecisiveness that an individual has by the location of the person on the axis. Depending on an individual's location, appropriate counseling strategies can then be identified. For example, if a person is located on the axis for indecision and indecisiveness, serious dysfunction would be indicated. This classification would call for "dealing with the anxiety, depression, low self-concept, or lack of decision-making skills that contribute to a specific client's indecisiveness" (see Fig. 6).

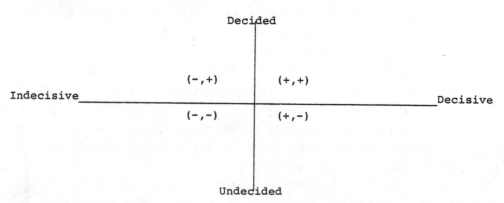

Figure 6. The Orthogonal Axes Representing the Decided-Undecided State and Decisive-Indecisiveness of Career Decision Making. *Personnel and Guidance Journal*, 62:637–639, 1984. Copyright 1984 by AACD. Reprinted with permission.

Holland and Holland (1977), Salomone (1982), and Tyler (1969) have also concluded that a person's indecisiveness concerning vocational goals reflects complex personality problems that may be reflected in maladaptive behavior.

Many job seekers who do enter into career counseling are not only undecided but also are indecisive. They tend to make very little progress in the vocational counseling process. Career counselors need to be aware of the high levels of anxiety that exist with indecisiveness. The anxiety, fear and resulting conflicts need to be dealt with through personal counseling before these job seekers can effectively use the special help that a placement counselor offers. Referral may be indicated if the career counselor does not have the training to counsel problems of such depth.

CONTRADICTIONS

Conflict is also expressed when job seekers make contradictory comments about aspects of their desired job goals during their interviews with the placement interviewer. Usually, their job goals are mentioned at the beginning of the interview and are explored in terms of what job vacancies are on file with the placement office. Many times, when the counselor begins to bring such job leads to their attention, the job seekers contradict their initial statements of job goal by mentioning a different goal. Usually, this occurs some time during the middle or at the end of the interview. It is illustrated by the following:

Placement	
Counselor:	Let me see. . . . Here's a job teaching Common Branches on Long Island. Didn't you say you were interested in the North Shore of Long Island?
Job Seeker:	Yes, I did. But . . . do you have any high school English jobs? I'd like it in New Jersey, so that I would be near my folks.

There is nothing in the literature that explains the dynamics that may be in operation. The statements suggest an inner conflict. It is possible that the presenting statement of job goal may be what the individual seeks as a result of the expectations of family and other influences from his or her social environment. However, when the seeming contradiction of goal is expressed, it may well be what the job seeker really desires. It is often expressed when he or she has established rapport with the interviewer.

Such contradictions may be understood in terms of Transactional Analysis theory (Berne, 1972). In this situation, the initial expression of job goal would be the effect of the "parent" rather than the "adult" within the individual. The expressed job goal has been molded by parental influences, whether or not they are recognized by the job seeker. If it were the effect of the "adult" ego state, the job goal would have been assessed objectively on the basis of experience and there would have been a firm commitment to the goal.

In this situation, the switch in job goal that was expressed during the interview represents the "child" within the individual. It is what the job seeker would like to do, and so it is expressed. In a real sense, there is an intraconflict between these two ego states.

Another example of a seeming contradiction illustrates that lack of occupational information can be another significant factor.

Job Seeker: I'd like to work in advertising.

Placement
Interviewer: Uh. . . . doing what?

Job Seeker: Well . . . I don't like writing so nothing that involves copy . . . and I'm not interested in editing. I don't really like details and checking words and grammar; that would bore me.

Placement
Interviewer: I think I'm confused . . . if you aren't interested in writing and editing, have you considered being an Account Executive or working in Traffic?

Job Seeker: No, I didn't realize there was anything else I could do. I don't know much about advertising. It just sounds glamorous to me.

The dialogue indicates that the job seeker seems to be expressing an unrealistic goal, as well as possible inner conflict, by indicating he does not want to do the type of work that he knows is performed in the field he desires. As a result of the interviewer's exploration, the job seeker realizes that he does not possess sufficient information about the field.

This phenomenon is puzzling when it occurs during a placement interview. It certainly suggests that the job seeker is exhibiting confusion and inner conflict. It is observed primarily in job seekers with the transitional and negative job-seeking behavior patterns. This is an area in which further investigation is needed before the operating dynamics can be identified.

SUMMARY

Whenever defensive and self-defeating behavior is exhibited, anxiety and fear are the underlying dynamics of avoidant behavior. Fear of success and fear of failure can be two contributing factors to indecision and indecisiveness concerning job goals. Job seekers exhibit a variety of defensive game behaviors, which are erected as invisible barriers but barriers, nevertheless, to vocational decision making. They are expressions of the individuals' defense mechanisms.

Understanding these defense mechanisms that job seekers exhibit in their behavior enables the placement counselors to identify appropriate counseling strategies that can help their clients to become increasingly effective in obtaining a job. Chapter Eight focuses on some of these counseling approaches.

Chapter Eight

COUNSELING APPROACHES

Through professional training and counseling experience, career and placement counselors develop for themselves philosophical counseling approaches that they use in helping the vocationally undecided individuals to crystallize their career direction and their job goals. This fact is the rationale for not spelling out the author's personal approach to counseling clients who exhibit a variety of difficulties in crystallizing personal job goals and who are unsuccessful in obtaining the jobs they desire. Actually, the author's counseling style is eclectic, in that its techniques are based on the Ginzberg, Super and Holland theories of vocational choice and development and on a variety of counseling approaches that have proven helpful with job seekers, depending on the depth of the problem exhibited in their job-seeking behavior pattern. The fabric of the counseling style of most vocational counselors undoubtedly is also eclectic.

Therefore, this chapter presents counseling approaches and suggests strategies that have evolved from several schools of counseling that counselors may wish to consider in their efforts with the vocationally undecided. Regardless of the age of the client, that person is a potential job seeker. The more realistic and clearly identified the job goal and the more self-actualized and independent the behavior of the individual at the time of seeking a job, the more effective he or she will be in obtaining a job. High school and college counselors can do much through their vocational counseling to help their clients to develop the characteristics of positive job-seeking behavior.

Since the 1970s a variety of forms of career assistance have developed that provide alternatives to individual career counseling and testing programs. These options include career planning courses, workshops and seminars, films, filmstrips, audio tapes and computer-based programs of career exploration, as well as internships and part-time jobs that can provide a firsthand exploratory experience in many different career fields and work settings.

The group counseling approaches were largely developed during the 1970s as a means of reaching more people who needed help at a time when there was need for institutional fiscal accountability because of the state of the economy, and career counseling and placement staffs became limited in size. The evidence from the literature is that these group interventions are effective in producing the desired outcome of developing the behaviors that lead to the specification of realistic career choices, depending on the size of the group, the number of sessions and the style of group leadership. Most of these interventions focus on developing exploration and decision-making skills.

Individual career counseling continues to be the preferred approach for many individuals seeking help in learning what they should do. Exploration for self-knowledge and career options and the assessment of these options for determining a career goal are also pursued effectively on a one-to-one basis.

COUNSELING DEFENSIVE BEHAVIOR

Individual counseling interventions enhance the possibilities for counselors to explore the effect of their clients' personal dynamics upon aspects of their vocational behavior. This is especially true when self-defensive behavior that stems from anxiety and conflict is exhibited. The counselor needs to help them cope with their anxieties, fears and conflicts.

Depending on the special training in psychological counseling of the career and placement counselor and the operating philosophy of the career planning and placement service, it may be possible for personal counseling to be incorporated into the vocational counseling. However, many placement staff counselors do not have psychological training and it is not the purview of most placement offices to be involved with personal counseling; therefore, a referral to clinical or counseling psychologists is necessary for individuals who exhibit defensive behavior. The psychologist can help these job seekers to develop an understanding of their inner conflicts which produce anxiety and defensive behavior. When referral is made, it may be desirable for the psychologist and the career or placement counselor to work together.

Clinical Counseling

Forer (1965) suggests that clinical appraisal is necessary in vocational counseling when the behavior of individuals is defensive and maladaptive as a result of deep internal conflicts. He states: "Ego defenses will be used somewhat to allay anxiety or deal with unconscious superego motives at the expense of attention to reality and other personal needs." These individuals also reject important aspects of self, such as abilities, interests and needs, so that they do not have an accurate and realistic perception of themselves.

Forer identifies as autistic other behaviors that are involved in making a vocational choice. In this condition, the ego is not integrated. The effort and motivation of individuals are focused inward in an attempt to develop an inner balance. Motivation is not directed outward toward successfully coping with reality situations.

Consequently, self-appraisal of attributes, performance and social relationships is impaired. He further states: "Skills may be used inappropriately; interests are not substantiated by skills or aptitudes nor by [the] recognition of the ineptitude. The vocational choice is largely a symptom, an unrealistic fantasy, and its pursuit often has disintegrative effects upon the client."

Forer indicates that the degree of defensiveness or autism will also have an impact on other kinds of vocational behaviors, such as acquiring occupational and self-knowledge, applying knowledge appropriately to work tasks, objectively appraising and accurately perceiving and interpreting situations in their social and work environments. When these dynamics are not brought into the individuals' conscious awareness, then the defenses and rejections of these individuals will continue to produce self-defeating and defensive behavior.

The behavior of a young sophomore psychology student, whom the author interviewed early in her career regarding his immediate goal of obtaining a children's therapist job, suggests strongly Forer's description of autistic vocational behavior. This job seeker was unaware of the unrealistic aspects of his qualifications for the job he sought, nor was he able to interpret and assimilate the job information regarding the employer's requirements for the position for which he wished to apply. When he was informed that the employer's requirements for doctoral training and clinical experience were the reality of the market for the field of psychological therapy, his only reply was, "Ah . . . but what *is* reality?" At the end of the interview, he still remained unaware that his immediate job goal was unrealistic and inappropriate for him at that moment in time. He was in pursuit of a fantasy.

As noted in Chapter Four, job seekers with negative job-seeking behavior characteristics are lacking in self-awareness, have inaccurate perceptions and denigrate their abilities, skills and experiences, so that they have pictures of themselves that are out of focus and unrealistic. Their personality dynamics produce passive, dependent behavior and a resistance to exploration which is exhibited in their behavior and a resistance to exploration which is exhibited in their lack of effort in choosing a job goal and in trying to procure a job. As a result, they appear to a placement interviewer to have self-defeating behavior, as indeed they do. Dynamically, they are exhibiting defensive behavior, the roots of which are based in the pathogenic aspects of the family milieu. A clinical counseling approach rather than vocational counseling is indicated as the strategy that may unlock the internal barriers that produce their defensive behavior. Usually, it is found that after working through their feelings with a psychologist, they can become more effective in coping with the tasks that lead to a vocational choice.

Some components of defensive behavior and its dynamics are also observed in the job seekers with the transitional job-seeking behavior pattern. As was noted in Chapter Five, their family environment contains some of the same pathogenic dynamics as that of those individuals with negative job-seeking behavior. However, their family environment in other aspects is similar to the family milieu of those with positive job-seeking behavior, so that they possess a core of health not present in individuals with the negative job-seeking behavior pattern. However, when anxiety, conflict, and defensive behavior are present, these job seekers may also be helped by the clinical counseling approach which will focus on the underlying personal dynamics of their behavior. When insight is achieved, they become increasingly capable of developing more effective job-seeking behavior.

Multimodal Career Counseling

Applicable to helping individuals to identify their self-defeating behaviors and the internal blocks that immobilize behavior is a multimodal behavior therapy model that is described by Smith and Southern (1980). It is based on Lazrus' BASIC ID Model. Problem area classifications are identified as: (1) behavior, (2) affect, (3) sensation, (4) imagery, (5) cognition, (6) interpersonal relations, and (7) drugs. When problem areas are determined by counselor and client, the counseling interventions that need to be used are also indicated by this problem identification process. The problem areas can be interdependent in terms of their effect upon behavior.

This system can be adapted for multimodal career counseling. It can be used to change ineffective job-seeking behavior, especially when this behavior is defensive and self-defeating. It can also be used to assist individuals with the development of those vocational tasks that they have not achieved when their internal barriers inhibit successful completion of the tasks involved in the vocational development process.

Job-Seeking Defensive Behavior

Job placement interviewers have identified specific examples of the self-defeating behavior which reflect the dynamics of conflict exhibited by job seekers. These examples may serve as cues or guidelines for identifying the defensive behaviors that need to be explored for personal counseling intervention. They are as follows:

1. The job seeker who informs the placement counselor that he or she has to have a job in Manhattan because of family reasons but who looks only at those job vacancies in his or her field from New Jersey, Westchester, Putnam and Dutchess counties and Eastern Pennsylvania, ignoring the appropriate vacancies that are reported from Manhattan employers.

2. The job seeker who states emphatically that he or she wants to work between Forty-Second Street and Fifty-Ninth Street and between Madison Avenue and Lexington Avenue in New York City, but, when told of a position related to the desired job goal on Third Avenue and Sixty-First Street, he or she becomes indignant and rigidly clings to the geographically prescribed locale, even though the job is within two blocks north and one block east of the preferred geographic location for work.

3. The job seeker whose expressed goal is a management training position, and who also has a qualifying background for such a job, but who looks only at clerical vacancies.

4. The college graduate who accepts a position that does not require a college degree, even though there are vacancies in the field that do require a degree, and then complains that his or her work is unchallenging.

5. The job seeker who has an interview with an employer for a job that

he or she desires but who responds in monosyllables to questions asked and does not actively participate in the interview.

6. The job seeker who, upon arrival at the employer's office for the arranged appointment, does not open the door but retreats to the lobby of the office building.

7. The job seeker who is consistently late for all appointments with the placement counselor or employer but who expresses an immediate need of a job.

8. The job seeker who verbally expresses contradictory statements about his or her job goal in terms of the job or the geographic location, etc., when talking to the placement interviewer about job vacancies.

9. The job seeker who wishes to know more about a type of work but who will not explore sources of information about it.

10. The job seeker who will not take responsibility for his or her career choice and who seeks others to make that choice.

11. The job seeker who will not take the responsibility for seeking a job and who expects others to "get me a job."

12. The individual who vascillates among career or job options in an approach-avoidance behavior syndrome and, therefore, is incapable of closure.

13. The individual who vascillates among job options in an approach-approach behavior syndrome and is incapable of closure, even after he or she attempts to assess and compare each job option.

14. The individual who seeks a job but exhibits avoidant behavior in the process of applying for that job.

COUNSELING IMPAIRED AND DELAYED VOCATIONAL DEVELOPMENT

Many job seekers are marginally effective in obtaining jobs, because they have delayed vocational development. They have not successfully mastered all of the vocational tasks in a given period of time that they are expected to have accomplished. This section reviews a variety of counseling approaches that may be used to help these job seekers to improve their exploration and decision-making skills and to develop their vocational maturity.

Counseling for Self-Responsibility

Inasmuch as individuals with negative job-seeking behavior place the responsibility on others for determining their job goals and obtaining jobs for them, one counseling approach can be to help them to develop self-awareness, self-acceptance and self-responsibility for their perceptions, feelings and behaviors. Two schools of therapy which address themselves to this particular personal development are Gestalt Therapy and Reality Therapy. Techniques have evolved from both of these schools that actively involve the individuals in focusing on their responsibility for the outcomes of their behavior. Hence, self-awareness of feelings, attitudes, motivations, needs and values are focused upon and this leads to self-knowledge. When these techniques are adapted to vocational problems, development of exploratory behavior and increase of vocational maturity can result.

It is not surprising, therefore, that group interventions should have evolved which are based on the tenets of Gestalt Therapy and Reality Therapy and which are successful in producing the desired outcomes of self-acceptance and self-responsibility. For the interested reader, the group work of Brandel (1982), Passons (1972), and Pickering, Vacc and Osborne (1983) will be of interest.

Butcher (1982) also recognizes that individuals must be ready to take responsibility for making their own career decisions before they can benefit from a group intervention that focuses on vocational task deficit skills. However, when individuals are blocked by internal conflicts that produce indecisiveness, they must have help in resolving these conflicts before they are able to profit from training in the decision-making process.

These individuals not only have a need to develop a self-identity but also to develop a vocational direction in context with their evolving sense of self. They also need to understand how self and vocational direction interrelate. Therefore, Butcher proposes that a counseling strategy for a group intervention with indecisive persons should be a dynamic interaction within the group in exploring and developing self-awareness of attributes. Self-perceptions are modified by this means as well as by assessments and feedback from the group. Knowledge is related to the world of work through exploration of values and personal styles, and planned decision making ensues as group participants take responsibility for applying their self-awareness to the consideration of their work options.

This approach can be an effective model with the indecisive because it enables the individual to develop responsibility for an awareness of abilities, skills and values, to interact cooperatively with others, and to begin to take more responsibility for decisions, so that life plans begin to be formulated with self-direction.

Developmental Career Counseling

Developmental career counseling is a widely used approach that is theoretically based on Super's (1957) theory of vocational development. It is concerned with the successful completion of the vocational developmental tasks that we expect to be completed in certain periods of time. Both Ginzberg (1951) and Super (1957) provide a framework that gives us a general timetable for when a vocational stage is normally completed. It is possible, therefore, to recognize delayed or retarded vocational development (see Chap. Six).

The developmental career counseling approach is helpful to individuals with characteristics of transitional job-seeking behavior who seem to have delayed vocational development. In individual counseling, they are frequently exploring to obtain self-knowledge and are identifying and evaluating viable career options in order to crystallize a career direction. All of these tasks need to be successfully completed before a specific and realistic job choice can be made.

According to Lunneborg (1983),[1] counselors work with the individuals' feelings, exploration of problems and their plans for action. Their counseling approach is nondirective in their responses to their counselees' emotions, in the clarification and in the working through of feelings, and in the consideration of possible actions that the clients might take. They are directive with counselees in response to their rational expressions, in setting topics for discussion, and in exploring factual data.

---

[1]Lunneborg, Patricia W.: Career counseling techniques. In Walsh, W. Bruce, and Osipow, Samuel H. (Eds.): *Handbook of Vocational Development.* (Hillsdale: Lawrence Erlbaum Associates, 1983, Vol. 2), pp. 41–76. Used with permission of Lawrence Erlbaum Associates and the author.

Group Counseling Approach

The basic concept concerning the importance of completing the expected vocational tasks before a realistic choice can be made has stimulated the development of group counseling interventions that are designed to accomplish this goal. Consequently, the focus is on the teaching of exploration and decision-making skills as part of career planning courses or workshops. There have been successful outcomes as a result of the group approach.

Exploratory Behavior. Aiken and Johnson (1973), Babcock and Kaufman (1976), Hazel (1976), Healy (1974), Jepson, Dustin and Miars (1982), Johnson, Johnson and Yates (1981), Mendonca and Siess (1976), Westbrook (1974), and Varvil-Weld and Fretz (1983) have indicated that an important effect of the group counseling intervention is the increase in exploratory behaviors of the participants during and after their group counseling experience.

Westbrook (1974) and Smith (1981) provide evidence that the structure of the group intervention and the style of the group leader's presentation have an effect on the outcomes of the group experience of the participants. This is important for counselors to note when planning group counseling sessions.

Exploratory behavior also is an important factor affecting the successful outcome of job interviews. Placement staffs have noted that those individuals who research companies that they plan to see when these companies make their recruiting visit to the college placement office tend to be the job applicants who are invited by the recruiters for additional interviews. They usually receive job offers as a result of their visits. Their knowledge about the company impresses the recruiter who usually shares this reaction with members of the placement staff. The significance of this empirical observation is supported by the recent research study of Stumpf, Austin and Hartman (1984).

Decision Making

Difficulty in making a vocational decision may be caused by a skill deficit rather than by the underlying dynamics of indecisiveness. When such is the case, decision-making skills can be taught in career planning courses and workshops, as well as in individual counseling sessions. The task of making decisions can be learned. The teaching approaches may be theoretically based in developmental behavioral counseling. Barker (1981), Cochran, Hetherington and Strand (1980), Donald and Carlisle (1983), Gillingham and Lounsbury (1979), Heppner and Krause (1979), McWhirter, Nichols and Banks (1984), Perovich and Mierzwa (1980), and Smith (1981) describe the effectiveness of the group counseling approach in developing the decision-making skills of individuals.

Barker (1981), Berger-Gross, Kahn and Weare (1983) and Rubinton (1980) identify the effect of the individual's style of decision making as an important factor in learning decision-making skills.

Rubinton's (1980) investigation on the effectiveness of the rational, intuitive and dependent styles of decision making with rational and intuitive interventions upon the certainty of career choices and the vocational maturity of college students indicated that a match of the decision-making styles with the comparable decision-making intervention was an important factor. Her findings indicated that the rational intervention was the most effective with persons who had the rational style of decision making. Their increase in certainty of choice and vocational maturity was even greater than was the increase made by individuals with the intuitive style of decision making who experienced the intuitive intervention approach. Persons with the dependent style actually decreased their vocational maturity and failed to develop decision-making skills when exposed to either the rational or intuitive intervention. They remained ineffective in decision-making skills. It should be noted that individuals with the dependent style of decision making strongly resemble individuals with the negative job-seeking behavior pattern.

Behavioral Counseling

The roots of behavioral counseling are in learning theory. When used on vocational problems, its focus is on changing behavior that has a negative effect on the successful obtainment of vocational goals. The behavior therapy techniques that are adapted for vocational counseling are (1) social modeling that usually involves the use of films or taped recordings to depict desired behaviors, (2) verbal reinforcement in which the counselor responds positively in both word and gesture to the desired behavior that the counselee exhibits, (3) assertive practice that rehearses the counselee by means of role playing to become more assertive, and (4) systematic desensitization to inhibit problem behaviors. The work of

John Krumboltz and Carl Thoresen are associated with this approach to vocational counseling.

Krumboltz and Schroeder (1965) developed two counseling approaches, which they termed "reinforcement counseling" and "model-reinforcement counseling," and tested their effectiveness in increasing the exploratory behavior necessary for effective decision making on a population of high school students.

Model-reinforcement counseling was the most effective approach with males which replicated the findings of Krumboltz and Thoresen (1964) in a previous study. They attribute this effect to the fact that the model tape used in these studies discussed only male interests and concerns which were not akin to female interests. Consequently, the reinforcement counseling approach was less effective with females. They also found that those students who were exposed to either of the two behavioral interventions exhibited significantly more information seeking behavior during the interview than did those students who did not experience the reinforcement and model-reinforcement counseling. These behavioral counseling techniques can be another effective approach for developing exploratory behavior.

Behavior Therapy Techniques and Job-Seeking Behavior

Techniques of behavior therapy have been adapted to help job seekers to become more effective in their efforts to find a job. Behavioral or assertive practice (assertiveness training) and modeling have been used for this purpose.

Krumboltz et al. (1979)[2] state that whatever behaviors are modeled and rehearsed, the frequency of the use of these behaviors is increased. He cites the significant increase in the presentation of skills and personal opinions of participants in a discussion group who were exposed to a filmstrip on job interview skills (modeling) and to a discussion of an article about interviewing (behavioral rehearsal). The group's superior gain in interview skills was the result of the behavioral techniques that were used.

The author has used the modeling and behavioral rehearsal tech-

---

[2]Krumboltz, John D., Becker-Haven, Jane F., and Burnett, Kent F.: Counseling psychology. *Annual Review of Psychology,* 30:553–602, 1979.

"Reproduced with permission from the *Annual Review of Psychology,* Volume 30, 1979 by Annual Reviews Inc.," and with permission of the senior author.

niques in group demonstrations of the characteristics exhibited in the positive and negative job-seeking behavior patterns to increase student awareness of behaviors exhibited in a job interview. Two student volunteers are coached in the characteristic response behavior of each pattern but are invited to develop their own "script" of responses for a vignette demonstration. A graduate student, a counselor, or a visiting employer usually plays the role of job interviewer. The vignettes are conducted for ten to fifteen minutes and are stopped when the "job interviewer" feels that the essence of each behavioral pattern has been demonstrated (modeling). The group is then asked which applicant they would hire if they were the employer. Without fail, they select the representative of the positive job-seeking behavior pattern. A discussion follows (behavioral rehearsal) in which the group explores how they felt as the demonstration was unfolding, and frequently they raise questions about the effect of personality dynamics on interview skills.

Assertion training can be effective in modeling behavior that is unassertive, according to Galassi and Galassi (1978), Krumboltz (1979), and LaFitte and Phillips (1980). It can be an effective technique in assisting job applicants to become more effective in job interviewing.

At the Ellen Morse Tishman Memorial Seminars—a ten-week workshop for women with family responsibilities who are returning to the world of work—at Hunter College, assertive practice in interviewing is included in these sessions. Many of the participants are hesitant to seek interviews in their networking for career information, and assertiveness training is introduced as a support for this activity. The effect of this training supports the findings of LaFitte and Phillips (1980) that assertiveness training is effective in developing positive job-interviewing skills. The group leader has observed that the Tishman seminar women gain confidence in reaching out for interviews and are more successful in getting the information they need from employers and professionals.

Paradoxical Approach

Lopez (1983) reports a paradoxical counseling technique used in individual counseling for individuals with indecision. It is a paradoxical approach based on the behavior therapy tenet that active practice of a behavior produces a fatigue response reaction. In this case, it results in the inhibition of the problem vocational behavior involved in being unable to make a choice. Self-defeating behaviors resulting from anticipatory anxiety can be modified as a result, so that the counselee is no longer blocked from taking effective action in the decision-making process. This is accomplished by having the counselee not make a vocational choice and resist pressure from others to do so. As a result, a fatigue response to the not making a choice does occur. Consequently, the individual is better able to make a vocational decision in time.

Trait-and-Factor Counseling

Initially, the Trait-Factor approach in vocational guidance was started in 1909 by Frank Parsons (1909) in his attempt to match people's traits to factors required in jobs. Today, an outstanding example of this approach is Holland's theory of vocational choice, which is based on the concept of the interrelationship between the individual's vocational personality and the work environment, and involves the matching of the individual with job and career goals that are related to his or her personality type. This is a useful concept for career counseling.

Holland's Theory

Holland's (1966, 1985) theory makes a special contribution to the understanding of aspects of job-seeking behavior. Six vocational personality types are identified as *Realistic, Intellectual,* (later renamed *Investigative*), *Social, Conventional, Enterprising* and *Artistic,* which interact with the individual's cultural, physical and social environments, so that the person develops ways of coping within the different work environments that correspond to his or her personality type. Consequently, the interaction of personality traits and characteristics within a type of model environment has a bearing on vocational behavior, including vocational choice, stability, achievement and satisfaction. When the individual's personality characteristics relate to the characteristics of a given model work environment, then there tends to be greater satisfaction and stable behavior exhibited in the career field that is chosen. This is because such an environment enables the individual to express abilities, attitudes, interests, skills and values and to become involved comfortably with problems and roles germane to the given environment.

The relationship of personality types and model environments is defined as follows (Holland, 1966):

There are six kinds of environments: Realistic, Intellectual [later renamed *Investigative*], *Social, Conventional, Enterprising, and Artistic.* Each environment is dominated by a given type of personality, and each environment is typified by physical settings posing special problems and stresses. For example, Realistic environments are "dominated" by Realistic types of people: that is, the largest percentage of the population in the environment resembles the Realistic type.

This also holds true for the Investigative, Social, Conventional, Enterprising and Artistic environments. They are also dominated by their respective personality types.

By means of the six personality types, Holland (1985) has developed a means for not only identifying the primary personality types but also the secondary and tertiary types, etc., that are part of a person's pattern. In this way, a pattern of resemblances to any of the six types can be identified that permits the complexities of any given personality to be considered and recognized in the solving of vocational-choice problems. This approach in using Holland's six categories gives a flexible identification system for a potential 720 personality patterns and coping behaviors. The personality patterns may be determined by such scales as the Vocational Preference Inventory, Self-Directed Search and certain scales in the Strong-Campbell Interest Inventory.

Holland's (1979) widely used Self-Directed Search (SDS) identifies an individual's combination of personality types which can be translated for appropriate occupations by matching the highest three codes for an individual with the same code combinations listed in the Occupational Finder code book. The identified occupations can then be explored. Based on the experience of the author, the SDS is an effective tool in career counseling, especially for those individuals who have not yet made a vocational decision and who are exploring their options from which they hope to make a choice.

The identification of their vocational personality patterns (the three typological codes that score the highest) increases their self-awareness in many instances. In other instances, it confirms for them what they have sensed about themselves. It stimulates discussion, either in individual counseling or in counseling groups, of the many factors that have contributed to and that are expressed in their patterns.

The SDS serves as a guideline for their career exploration. They start out exploring the occupations that match their code pattern, as well as those occupations that match at least two of the three of the codes. These alternate possibilities can give them a modicum of satisfaction. In reading career information about these occupations, the individuals can relate the meaningful activity focus of their patterns to the focus of the tasks that are described in the occupational material about many career areas. In so doing, they can identify other career options that may also be viable for them. In this sense, it is a useful tool for the decision-making process.

It has been the author's experience that use of the SDS tends to be the catalyst that moves many counselees into the process of career exploration. Occasionally, job seekers seem to find that it is more comfortable to get started with the exploration task when they have a direction to follow that is structured on the rationale of their identified Holland codes. Not knowing where to start exploring among the occupational families can be an overwhelming experience for many. Therefore, they tend not to get started with this important task that is necessary for realistic decision making. In this sense, Holland's SDS scale is an effective tool in the counseling process that assists in developing positive job-seeking behavior.

Holland (1985) also states that when there is knowledge about an individual's personality and work environment type, it is possible to make vocational predictions concerning choice of vocation, changes of job and vocational achievements. He identifies four factors concerning the types of personality and work environment that can affect such predictions. They are as follows:

1. *Consistency.* Some types of personality and environment are more similar than are other types in regard to their characteristics. For example, the Realistic and Investigative types resemble each other, as do the Social and Enterprising. However, the Conventional and Artistic do not resemble each other, nor do the Realistic and Social, nor the Investigative and Enterprising. Therefore, when there is a relationship between two types in the individual's personality pattern, vocational predictions would tend to be more reliable than when there is not a relationship between two types in the individual's personality pattern. This is Holland's hexagonal model that defines the degree of consistency among personality patterns.

2. *Differentiation.* When the individual's personality most closely resembles only one of the personality types, it is more clearly defined than when the individual's personality type resembles two or more of the six personality types. A vocational personality that is clearly defined leads to adaptive career development. However, when the pattern is not consistent and differentiated, maladaptive career development results.

3. *Identity.* Identity refers to the individual who has specifically defined abilities, interests and goals which do not fluctuate. It also applies to a work environment that has specific integrated tasks, goals and rewards over a long period of time.

4. *Congruence.* The relationship between a personality type and its corresponding environment is an important factor for the satisfaction of the individual, in that the person is able to find the type of work opportunity and rewards that he or she is seeking. However, when the personality type and the work environment type are not similar, personal satisfactions in work are not found. This happens when work environment and personality types are incongruent.

The placement interviewer has observed often that some of his or her clients who return to the placement office for job leads while still employed express distaste for their work and boredom with their jobs. Inevitably, when their vocational personality types have been identified by means of the Self-Directed Search (SDS), it has been found that the relationship of the individual's vocational personality and work environment is incongruent. No satisfaction in work is attained because the work environment does not meet the person's needs, nor does it provide an outlet for the use of the person's competencies and interests. Identification of the client's personality type enables the exploration of more appropriate job options and work environments that will be congruent with the individual's vocational personality type. When such a situation occurs, the client usually is not only relieved to find the answer to his or her vocational dissatisfaction but also is motivated to explore and assess new job options.

It has also been observed by placement counselors that when there is consistency of personality types exhibited in the client's vocational personality pattern, there tends to be satisfaction with the work tasks of the job when the work environment also has a matching combination of types.

Job seekers who have the best-formed sense of identity are those with the characteristics of positive job-seeking behavior. They have identified their abilities, interests and goals. They also succeed in obtaining the jobs that they seek.

The four vocational personality factors of consistency, differentiation, identity and congruence have been identified by Holland as guidelines for counselor assessment of the individual. In a very real sense they can be used as a diagnostic tool for the counselor to use in identifying the type of intervention that is needed to help his or her client.

Holland's theory (1985) also identifies maladaptive career development as a result of a vocational personality that is not clearly defined and which tends to be neither consistent nor differentiated. This holds true for individuals who resemble inconsistent vocational personality types, the difficulty being that there is not a relationship with work environment models.

Other causes of maladaptive or stunted career development are varied. It may be the effect of psychological dynamics or impaired and delayed vocational development as has been previously discussed. However, it also may be the result of the individual's limited experience that contributes to lack of self-knowledge and lack of knowledge about work environments. The placement counselor usually can rectify this situation by helping the person to obtain such information by means of self-assessment, career exploration, visits to work environments, internships and carefully selected part-time jobs that will give him or her an awareness of work environments in a variety of settings. By means of these interventions, the individual can compensate for the information deficits that he or she possesses and can develop an understanding about self and the world of work.

Reality-Based Counseling Approach

Gottfredson's (1981, 1984) theoretical approach to counseling is applicable to both individual and group interventions. Her (1981) developmental theory which integrates psychological and sociological factors with vocational development can provide the counselor with insight into the client's problem of making either a realistic vocational choice or career change. It is concerned with the antecedents of occupational aspirations and covers four stages of self-concept development between the ages three and fourteen and over.

Gottfredson's Stages of the Self-Concept

The first stage (Gottfredson, 1981) is that of *Orientation to Size and Power* (ages 3–5) in which children develop an awareness of what it is to be an adult. The next stage is *Orientation to Sex Roles* (ages 6–8). During this stage orientation to occupations in concrete terms is based on external observable behaviors. It is at this period of time that an awareness of an occupation's appropriateness to gender self-concept forms. The next developmental stage is *Orientation to Social Valuation* (ages 9–13) in which a self-concept of social class and ability develops. Both of these factors have an effect on recognizing occupations that are either appropriate or inappropriate to consider because of family expectations, or because of the effort involved when the ability necessary for such an occupation is not possessed. The final stage is the *Orientation to the Internal, Unique Self* in which feelings, interests and values are identified and considered.

Factors Affecting Vocational Choice

As a result of these evolving stages of self-concept development, the individual eliminates or tentatively chooses occupational options on the basis of his or her perception of appropriateness to gender, ability, social class and prestige. Vocational goals are shaped by these factors and are formed by means of the individual's (1) perception of personal traits, (2) development of preferences evolving from new awareness of self, (3) perceived need to compromise between what he or she would like to do and what is possible to do as a result of the labor market, and (4) integration of crystallized occupational preferences into a conceived life plan.

Implications for Counseling

Gottfredson's theory also has implications for career counseling, especially where the counselee is undecided and/or where seemingly inappropriate career choices seem to have been made. Anxiety regarding choice is often a resulting dynamic.

Certainly, the career counselor in helping his or her counselees to make career choices focuses on their abilities, interests and values by means of tests, exercises, exploration and discussion. However, Gottfredson's theory, supported by vocational research studies, indicates that vocational choice is early rooted in and strongly related to an individual's gender, social class and intelligence. In career counseling there generally tends not to be a consideration of the effect that gender and social class may have upon the individual's dynamic process in considering vocational options.

Gottfredson makes a cogent point. It is often on the basis of ability and interest that vocational choices are deemed to be unrealistic by the counselor. These choices often can be explained in terms of the effect of the clients' perception of gender. However, many occupations that may seem to be appropriate on the basis of interests, abilities and values may be rejected by counselees who perceive an occupation to be unsuitable in terms of their perception of what is appropriate work for their gender.

Social background also has an effect. Individuals may express both interest and commitment to occupational goals that require less intellectual ability than they have exhibited in school and on tests. This can be the influence that a lower socioeconomic background has in not motivating higher career goal expectations. On the other hand, there are those who have chosen goals that require a higher level of intellectual ability that is necessary for success than they actually have, and these goals too may not be supported by the counselees' measured interests. This may be the influence of a middle-class background which has raised their expectations to obtain jobs in career fields that are difficult for them to enter. In both these instances, such career choices could undoubtedly be considered to be unrealistic by career counselors, especially if they are unaware of the effect that social background may have upon the individual.

As a result of the effect that gender and social background have upon individuals, counselees may also exhibit difficulties with alternative options for career fields and job levels. Their personal career preferences may not meet their abilities and interests, and they may express conflicting goals as a result.

These individuals can be helped by the counselor who does not take for granted the components involved in the decision-making process. When exploring aptitudes, interests, skills and values, the counselor's awareness of the counselees' concept of work which is appropriate to their gender and to their social class can help assist them to make realistic decisions about career and job goals.

Reality-Based Exploration System

Gottfredson (1984) is also concerned about the counseling approach that the vocational counselor uses in helping clients to develop realism when crystallizing career goals and making vocational decisions. There are two tasks in this process upon which she focuses. One is the expansion of the clients' vocational options for consideration. This may be especially true for those clients who are socially or economically disadvantaged. The other task is helping clients with the realism of their vocational decisions. This may be difficult when the clients' goals are unrealistic and especially difficult when the clients' goals may be tinged with wish fulfillment.

Gottfredson feels that although these tasks may represent conflicting demands for some counselors, they do not need to do so. She presents a system for counseling that encourages the increase in the clients' exploration of career choices, as well as the development of reality in their vocational decisions.

Criteria for Realism

Gottfredson identifies two criteria for determining realism of a vocational choice as being the suitability of the chosen occupation for a given individual and the accessibility of jobs in that occupation in the labor market. Determined suitability and accessibility can be tools for the counselor to use in assessing the realism of a counselee's crystallized vocational goal.

Suitability of Career Choice. Suitability can be indicated to a certain degree by the counselee's measured interests and abilities. This knowledge about self is a foundation for realism of career choice. Another very important tool is the knowledge about the counselee's vocational personality type.

By using Holland's (1985) Vocational Personality Types and his corresponding Work Environments (described above), together with Gottfredson's (1984) Occupational Aptitude Patterns (OAP) Map, an assessment of suitability can be formulated by the counselor for his or her clients. Gottfredson has devised a thirteen-cluster Occupational Aptitude Patterns Map by abstracting and clustering similar job attributes from the United States Employment Service's (USES) research data on sixty-six USES occupational aptitude groups, which cover the major percentage of jobs in the labor market. By clustering job attributes, her thirteen OAP clusters show both similarities and dissimilarities of job activity focus for a large variety of occupations. They also have a relationship to Holland's (1985) hexagonal model of the interrelatedness of environmental types.

Accessibility of Jobs. Accessibility of jobs in the labor market is the other criterion of realism in vocational choice. Gottfredson (1984) acknowledges that this information can be difficult for a counselor to possess. However, the author wishes to suggest ways in which information concerning the supply and demand for workers in the labor market may be obtained.

Interviewers in the field of job placement, whether they be in a college placement service or the United States Employment Service, literally have their thumb on the pulse of the labor market. This is because of the large volume of jobs that these interviewers handle every day in their efforts to help people find jobs. A phone call to a placement service for information about jobs and career fields will obtain the needed information. Placement interviewers can usually provide data on changing job requirements, volume of jobs received, salary ranges, etc., for a wide variety of occupations.

Data on the trends of different occupations can also be obtained from the Bureau of Labor Statistics and can be very useful in predicting accessibility of jobs in the future. A caution should be noted, however, regarding *any* occupational forecast. It should be realized that the forecast is a good prediction only as long as the factors upon which the forecast is based hold constant. For example, in the past ten years and within a very short span of time, the economy fluctuated between a large supply and a short supply of engineers. A factor that undoubtedly contributed to the dearth of trained engineers at a time of increased demand for them was the fact that there had not been many engineering jobs available in the labor market; as a result, fewer men and women elected to study engineering. Since there are factors beyond our control that influence labor market changes, many industries are cyclical in nature. Consequently, forecasts cannot be set in stone, although they are useful tools when used knowledgeably and when the events and conditions upon which they are based are also understood.

A factor that is not too frequently considered when assessing the availability of jobs is the natural attrition of workers due to health, retirement, change of jobs and death. These factors need to be kept in mind when the counselees' job choices seem to be suitable according to their aptitudes and their interests, but when projected employment opportunities appear to be limited. In a sense, there can be a well of "hidden" accessibility of jobs that is unpredictable when making projections.

System for Realistic Exploration

Gottfredson (1984) presents a system that the counselor may use in helping his or her clients explore vocational options that introduces the quality of realism into their career considerations. She identifies ten steps in the process in which both the counselor and counselee actively participate. The counselor's role is to assess the counselee's aptitudes, interests, special circumstances and goals, and to introduce the OAP clusters and the exploration process to the counselee. The counselee then ranks the OAP clusters to obtain his or her most preferred fields or "foci" of work; identifies levels of work that seem to be suitable in terms of his or her abilities, interests and feelings of prestige levels; selects with the counselor several OAP clusters for exploration; and lists a few occupational titles from within those clusters for further exploration, which are reviewed with the counselor. At this point, the counselor may introduce for consideration similar occupational titles found in other OAP clusters. The counselee then evaluates the suitability and accessibility of occupations under consideration, identifies his or her best possibilities, how his or her competitive edge might be improved and makes contingency plans to be put into operation. The counselor's role then is to evaluate how successful the counselee's exploration has been and to suggest other steps to be taken if they are deemed to be necessary.

This system is structured so that realism is a component of the vocational exploration process. It enhances the possibility that realistic job goals will be made. It can be an effective approach in career counseling when the counselor is concerned with helping his or her counselees to consider viable career options that are realistic for them to pursue in their life plans.

Gottfredson's theory and reality-based exploration system are yet another approach to helping job seekers develop crystallized goals that are realistic. When this is accomplished, then the job seekers possess a major characteristic of positive job-seeking behavior. The probability of obtaining a position in a relatively short period of time, compared to those with the characteristics of transitional and negative job-seeking behavior, is enhanced.

SUMMARY

A variety of counseling approaches have been identified in this chapter that may be useful to placement counselors and interviewers in working with individuals who have ineffective job-seeking behavior.

Individuals with negative job-seeking behavior exhibit defensive behavior which results from distorted perceptions, anxiety, fear and conflict. This maladaptive vocational behavior can have its roots in neuroticism and pathology stemming from the individual's perception of his or her early social environment. A clinical approach to counseling such behavior is mentioned for such problems in the citing of Forer's (1965) approach and the BASIC ID approach (Smith and Southern, 1980). The Behaviorist approaches of Krumboltz (1964, 1965, 1979) and Lopez (1983) are also cited as another system that can be helpful with some clients who are incapable of making vocational decisions. Career counseling, per se, for such individuals tends to be ineffective until they have developed an awareness of their inner dynamics which cause their self-defeating behavior.

Individuals with the transitional job-seeking behavior pattern need help in developing their exploration and decision-making skills. Therefore, other counseling approaches are mentioned. The Developmental counseling approaches are frequently effective. When there is evidence that clients are unable to crystallize vocational choices because of their failure to have successfully completed earlier vocational tasks, such as the task of exploration, Holland's (1966, 1985) identification of the relationship between vocational personality types and work environments, and Gottfredson's (1981, 1984) reality-based exploration system, offer counseling approaches that are effective in helping counselees to identify satisfying and realistic job career goals. These approaches include group counseling modalities which are effective with many individuals in developing these skills that are so essential for coping successfully with the vocational task of choosing a vocational goal.

APPENDICES

A COUNSELOR'S GUIDE TO DEFINITIONS OF CATEGORIES AND TOPIC AREAS OF PLACEMENT READINESS SCALE FOR JOBS IN EDUCATION

(5)

SPECIFICATION: Any response or question which indicates the client knows definitely what he or she wants and states this in specific and/or descriptive terms.

JOB DESIRED (I): Any response or question which indicates job title showing the client knows definitely what position he or she desires.

FIELD DESIRED (II): Any response or question which indicates the client has decided definitely what specific field he or she is interested in considering for employment.

LEVEL DESIRED (III): Any response or question which indicates the client has decided definitely which level or levels he or she is interested in considering for employment.

JOB REQUIREMENTS (IV): Any response or question which indicates the client has met, or is about to meet in time for consideration by an employer, requirements of certification, degrees, or experience for a desired position.

GEOGRAPHIC LOCATION (V): Any response or question which indicates the client has decided definitely on a specific geographic area or areas for considering job opportunities.

JOB APPLICATION (VI): Any response or question which indicates the client has developed procedures of job application, letter writing, interview skills, and is aware of their effectiveness in approaching an employer.

JOB CAMPAIGN (VII): Any response or question which indicates the client has developed procedures of a personal job campaign, or of a resume format, and is aware of their effectiveness in approaching an employer.

SALARY (VIII): Any response or question which indicates the client states specifically what salary he or she definitely desires.

REGISTRATION FORMS (IX): Any response or question which indicates that the client knows how he or she wishes to fill out forms, what he or she wishes to say about his or her professional objective, and what part of his or her background the client wishes to emphasize for the job goal the client has specified.

REFERENCE FORMS (X): Any response or question which indicates that the client knows from whom he or she wishes to obtain professional references and has distributed them or is in the process of distributing them.

(4)

CRYSTALLIZATION: Any response or question which indicates the client seeks to organize information and to evaluate and assess alternate choices as they relate to his or her background and the job market in order to determine the most advantageous choice.

JOB DESIRED (I): Any response or question which defines a desired position in terms of duties or responsibilities rather than by specific job titles.

FIELD DESIRED (II): Any response or question which indicates the client has assessed opportunities in a field or fields and is attempting to clarify his or her primary interest or goal in terms of these opportunities and his or her qualifications.

LEVEL DESIRED (III): Any response or question which indicates the client is attempting to clarify factors involved in making a personal preference for a given level.

JOB REQUIREMENTS (IV): Any response or question which indicates the client is in the process of attempting to meet requirements of certification, degrees, or experience for a desired position.

GEOGRAPHIC LOCATION (V): Any response or question which indicates the client is attempting to clarify factors in making a decision for considering job opportunities in a given geographic locale.

JOB APPLICATION (VI): Any response or question which indicates the client seeks evaluation of job application procedures for their effectiveness in approaching an employer.

JOB CAMPAIGN (VII): Any response or question which indicates the client is seeking evaluation of personal job campaign procedures or of resume format for effectiveness in approaching an employer.

SALARY (VIII): Any response or question which indicates the client is attempting to establish a range of salary he or she can consider for a new position.

REGISTRATION FORMS (IX): Any response or question which indicates that the client is in the process of evaluating how he or she wishes to fill out the forms, what he or she wishes to say about his or her professional objective, what part of his or her background he or she wishes to emphasize for the job desired, or client offers to make changes on forms that he or she feels will improve presentation of his or her background.

REFERENCE FORMS (X): Any response or question which indicates that the client is evaluating from whom it would be best to get a professional reference. References have been, or are, in the process of being distributed and the client offers to obtain additional references.

(3)

EXPLORATION: Any response or question in which the client seeks information to help him or her reach a decision.

JOB DESIRED (I): Any response or question which indicates that the client has done preliminary thinking regarding a specific position but requires additional information on job trends and opportunities before making decisions.

FIELD DESIRED (II): Any response or question which indicates that the client is thinking of fields primarily as those in which he or she is certified or is seeking information for a comparison of placement opportunities, even though the client may not have crystallized this field of primary interest.

LEVEL DESIRED (III): Any response or question which indicates the client has done preliminary thinking about the level of desired position but is investigating job analysis comparisons and teaching differences on various levels.

JOB REQUIREMENTS (IV): Any response or question which indicates that the client has done preliminary thinking about the desired job but seeks information on requirements for working on different levels, such as certification, degrees, and experiences.

GEOGRAPHIC LOCATION (V): Any response or question which indicates a need for information on job opportunities in specific geographic areas.

JOB APPLICATION (VI): Any response or question which indicates the client seeks knowledge on writing letters of application for, or on procedures in applying to, a specific given job lead, and where the client seeks information and help in thinking through the best possible procedures to use.

JOB CAMPAIGN (VII): Any response or question which indicates a lack of knowledge about planning a personal job campaign of his or her field, job resume and mechanics of its format.

SALARY (VIII): Any response or question in which information is sought because of a lack of information about salary schedules.

REGISTRATION FORMS (IX): Any response or question in which the client seeks information on how to interpret forms so he or she will know what information concerning the client's background would be best to emphasize, what the client wishes to say about professional objectives, and how the client should fill out the forms or indicates willingness to make additions and changes in forms which the interviewer suggests.

REFERENCE FORMS (X): Any response or question in which the client seeks information as to who should be asked for a professional reference or agrees to get new or additional references on file.

(2)

CONFUSION: Any response or question in which the client has not reached any definite decision concerning a specific desire but tends to present his or her interest in broad or vague terms without having given indication of having thought it through realistically to the point of making a specific choice.

JOB DESIRED (I): Any response or question in which the client states his or her job interest in vague or even in conflicting terms, indicating that he or she has not thought a choice through to the point of identifying his or her primary interest.

FIELD DESIRED (II): Any response or question which indicates that the client is thinking broadly of fields without giving any indication of having evaluated personal qualifications that may meet the requirements of job opportunities in these fields.

LEVEL DESIRED (III): Any response or question in which the client indicates breadth of interest without being able to specify any choice.

JOB REQUIREMENTS (IV): Any response or question which indicates the client is unaware of how to meet requirements of certification, degrees, or experience necessary for a job in his or her field of interest.

GEOGRAPHIC LOCATION (V): Any response or question which indicates the client is unable to specify a definite geographic area where he or she would consider employment, but states his or her geographic preference in such broad and vague terms as not to be meaningful.

JOB APPLICATION (VI): Any response or question which indicates lack of knowledge in writing letters of application or about procedures for applying for jobs.

JOB CAMPAIGN (VII): Any response or question which indicates the client has considered, but not started, a personal job campaign, nor has the client developed a resume.

SALARY (VIII): Any response or question which indicates the client has not decided what salary range he or she will accept, or in which a salary is demanded way above what the market offers for his or her training and experience.

REGISTRATION FORMS (IX): Any response or question which indicates that the client appeals for help in knowing what part of his or her background to emphasize, what he or she should say pertaining to his or her professional objective, or indicates that he or she sees no need to make any changes on registration forms suggested by the interviewer.

REFERENCE FORMS (X): Any response or question which indicates the client does not know to whom he or she should distribute references, or in which the client is selecting personal rather than professional references, or states that references which he or she has distributed should already be on file when advised that they have not been received.

(1)

PASSIVITY: Any response or question in which the client is placing the burden of decision or of action on someone else, where he or she seems to be unable to decide what he or she wants, or is unable to initiate action for himself or herself in meeting job requirements and seeking out job opportunities.

JOB DESIRED (I): Any response or question in which the client expresses job choice only in broad and vague terms and in which he or she attempts to place the burden of decision on someone else.

FIELD DESIRED (II): Any response or question in which the client is thinking broadly or vaguely of fields and attempts to place the burden of decision on someone else for evaluating his or her qualifications for opportunities in these fields.

LEVEL DESIRED (III): Any response or question in which the client is unable to make specific decisions for himself or herself and attempts to place the burden of decision on someone else.

JOB REQUIREMENTS (IV): Any response or question which indicates the client is unaware of the necessity of fulfilling the requirements for entrance into any field.

GEOGRAPHIC LOCATION (V): Any response or question which indicates that the client attempts to place the burden of decision about where to work on someone else.

JOB APPLICATION (VI): Any response or question where the client indicates lack of knowledge in making application for jobs and where he or she attempts to place the burden of initial action on someone else.

JOB CAMPAIGN (VII): Any response or question which indicates the client has never considered a personal job campaign or a resume.

SALARY (VIII): Any response or question which indicates the client has not considered what salary range he or she will accept and in which he or she appeals to someone else to make the decision.

REGISTRATION FORMS (IX): Any response or question which indicates the client is unable to organize background for recording on the registration forms in support of his or her job application, or indicates that he or she would prefer not to fill out new registration forms at all.

REFERENCE FORMS (X): Any response or question which indicates the client expects the placement service to distribute references for him or her, or indicates that he or she would prefer not to get references covering current experience.

A COUNSELOR'S GUIDE TO DEFINITIONS OF CATEGORIES AND TOPIC AREAS OF PLACEMENT READINESS SCALE FOR JOBS OTHER THAN IN EDUCATION

(5)

SPECIFICATION: Any response or question which indicates the client knows definitely what he or she wants and states this in definite terms.

JOB DESIRED (I): Any response or question which indicates the client knows definitely what position he or she desires.

> Examples: "I want to be a programmer."
> "I want to be a pharmaceutical salesperson."

FIELD DESIRED (II): Any response or question which indicates the client has decided definitely what specific field he or she is interested in considering for employment.

> Examples: "I want to be working in the sciences."
> "I want to be a lab technician" (by implication—science).
> "I'm interested in management."

LEVEL DESIRED (III): Any response or question which indicates that the client has decided definitely which level(s) he or she is interested in considering employment.

> Example: "...would consider starting as a secretary (skilled), if I could work into being an assistant-to-an-editor" (preprofessional).

JOB REQUIREMENTS (IV): Any response or question which indicates the client has met, or is about to meet in time for the employer to be able to consider him or her, those requirements of certification, licensing, degrees or experiences demanded for the desired job.

> Example: "By June I'll have the 24 credits in accounting which qualifies me for the Internal Revenue Agent."

GEOGRAPHIC LOCATION (V): Any response or question which indicates the client has decided definitely on a specific geographic area or areas for considering job opportunities.

Examples: "I want a job in Washington."

"... interested in N.Y. Met. area, that is, Westchester, L.I."

JOB APPLICATION (VI): Any response or question which indicates the client has developed procedures of job application, letter writing, interview skills, and is aware of their effectiveness with employers.

Examples: "I sent my resume to YZ, and it got me an interview."

"I spelled out what I did on my part-time job when I saw the interviewer.

"... was impressed I had related experience."

JOB CAMPAIGN (VII): Any response or question which indicates the client has developed procedures or a personal job campaign and is aware of his or her effectiveness in approaching employers.

Examples: "I went through the Market Research Directory for NYC firms, and I've been contacting them myself."

"I'm attending the physics convention ... figure I can look over the exhibits and make contact with employers."

SALARY (VIII): Any response or question which indicates the client knows specifically what salary he or she definitely desires.

Example: "I want $400 a week."

REGISTRATION FORMS (IX): Any response or question which indicates the client knows what he or she wishes to say about his or her professional objective; what part of his or her background he or she wishes to emphasize for the job goal he or she specifies.

Example: "I mentioned what I did for the House Plan Project under the extracurricular activities section, because that's got something to do with my goal."

REFERENCE FORMS (X): Any response or question which indicates the client knows to whom he or she wishes to give his or her reference forms to obtain a professional reference.

Example: "I'm giving my reference to be filled out by Professor X in the Math Department."

(4)

CRYSTALLIZATION: Any response or question that indicates the client has an idea of what he or she wants to do in descriptive terms, and that he or she seeks to organize information and to evaluate and to assess alternate choices as they may be related to his or her background and the job market in order to determine the most advantageous choice.

JOB DESIRED (I): Any response or question which defines a desired position in terms of duties or responsibilities rather than by a specific job title.

> Examples: "I want a job where I can work with math theory."
> "I'm pretty good at arranging things for the sorority, and I can usually smooth out difficulties with people. . . . I think I'd like something administrative. . . . I think I could handle it."

FIELD DESIRED (II): Any response or question which indicates the client has assessed opportunities in a field or fields and is attempting to clarify his or her primary interest in terms of these opportunities for which he or she has qualifications for consideration by an employer.

> Example: "I know I want a job which will let me help people . . . (service field) as a result of my field experience, I'm comfortable working with people with real problems . . . like in that agency. I like office work, too. . . . I think personnel jobs would be good for me."

LEVEL DESIRED (III): Any response or question which indicates the client is attempting to clarify his or her primary interest in terms of those opportunities for which he or she has qualifications for consideration by the employer.

> Example: "You need an M.S.W. degree for social work. . . . I'd do best to consider a case aide" (preprofessional).

JOB REQUIREMENTS (IV): Any response or question in which the client indicates he or she is making plans to meet requirements for certification, degrees, experience, etc., for a desired position.

> Example: " . . . in order to take the second actuarial test, I'll take the statistics course I need in night school next term, even though I'll have graduated in January."

GEOGRAPHIC LOCATION (V): Any response or question which indicates that the client is attempting to clarify factors in making a decision about locale of desired job.

> Example: "I want to go to grad school, so I guess I must consider a

job in any large city where there would be a graduate school."

JOB APPLICATION (VI): Any response or question which indicates that the client is evaluating job application procedures for their effectiveness in approaching an employer.

>   Example: "Considering the shortness of time, I suppose it would be better for me to phone for an appointment rather than write for it."

JOB CAMPAIGN (VII): Any response or question which indicates that the client is evaluating job campaign procedures for their effectiveness in approaching an employer.

>   Example: "I got pretty good results from sending this two-page resume out to companies in the *Placement Annual.* . . . At least I got some interviews lined up. I didn't get much of a response from just sending a letter without the details of my background. Guess that's how I should proceed."

SALARY (VIII): Any response or question which indicates that the client is evaluating factors in order to establish a salary range he or she can consider in approaching an employer.

>   Example: " . . . $225 a week minimum . . . I'm living at home now. . . . "

REGISTRATION FORMS (IX): Any response or question which indicates the client is in the process of evaluating his or her background for what is appropriate in his or her background to record on the registration forms to help the client attain the desired goal, or he or she offers to make changes on the forms which will present more appropriate information for the employer to consider.

>   Example: "I did all the advertising for our House Plan Project and handled the ads for our newspaper. . . . It might be good for me to list these responsibilities specifically on the forms so that it will show I've had indirectly related experience."

REFERENCE FORMS (X): Any response or question which indicates that the client is evaluating from whom it would be best to get a professional reference.

>   Example: "Since I want industrial sales, one from my own clients

(has own business) would be good to show how I can handle the public."

(3)

EXPLORATION: Any response or question which indicates that the client seeks out information to help him or her reach a decision.

JOB DESIRED (I): Any response or question which indicates that the client seeks information on job trends, requirements and opportunities, before making decisions.

Examples: "What jobs are open to me in the field of math?"
"What kind of jobs are in sales?"

FIELD DESIRED (II): Any response or question which indicates that the client is seeking information for a comparison of job opportunities even though he or she may not have crystallized the field of interest.

Example: "What is open to me? I'm a history major."

LEVEL DESIRED (III): Any response or question which indicates that the client is seeking information about the level of desired positions and is investigating a job analysis comparison or differences of working on different levels.

Example: "Suppose I did start as a secretary in a copywriting department . . . would that be better than to start as an advertising trainees, if what I want is copywriting?"

JOB REQUIREMENTS (IV): Any response or question which indicates that the client seeks information on the requirements for working in different jobs such as certification, degrees, experience, etc.

Examples: "To be a case aide, do I need an M.S.W.?"
"How can I qualify for a GS rating?"

GEOGRAPHIC LOCATION (V): Any response or question which indicates that the client seeks information about job possibilities in specific geographic locations.

Examples: "I want a social work job in Putney, VT."
"I prefer working in the New York area."

JOB APPLICATION (VI): Any response or question which indicates that the client seeks information about writing letters of application or on procedures on how to apply for a job.

Examples: "How do I write a letter applying for job? What do I say?"

"What can I expect from the interview? How do I start? What's the interviewer apt to say?"

JOB CAMPAIGN (VII): Any response or question which indicates that the client is seeking information on how to conduct a job campaign.

Examples: "How can I go on a job campaign of the companies I'm interested in?"

"I don't know how to set up a resume. Would you show me?"

SALARY (VIII): Any response or question which indicates that the client seeks information about salary scales.

Examples: "What can a bachelor's degree expect to get in the field of chemistry . . . a M.S.?"

"What salary could I expect in publishing . . . as an assistant to an editor . . . a proofreader?"

REGISTRATION FORMS (IX): Any response or question which indicates that the client seeks information on how to interpret his or her background for filling out the forms, asks questions about how to use the forms and what items on the forms mean.

Example: "I don't know what to put down under the category honors. Would the Mathematics Honor Society be the kind of thing?"

REFERENCE FORMS (X): Any response or question which indicates that the client seeks information about who should be asked for a professional reference or inquires into the reason for references and the use made of references.

Examples: "Whom should I ask? Someone in the Physics Department?"

"Can these references be used for graduate school?"

(2)

CONFUSION: Any response or reference which indicates that the client has not reached a definite decision concerning a specific job choice, but tends to present his or her interests in broad and vague terms without having given indication of having thought through realistically the factors affecting his or her choice, so that he or she is unable to make a specific, definite choice.

JOB DESIRED (I): Any response or question which indicates that the client states his or her job interest in broad, vague terms, and sometimes in conflicting statements, indicating that he or she has not thought a "choice" through to the point of identifying a specific primary interest.

>   Examples: "... something maybe working with people ... I don't know ... I just love helping people."
>   "... something in the math field ... I'm not good at details ... nothing with figuring."

FIELD DESIRED (II): Any response or question which indicates that the client is thinking vaguely or broadly of fields without giving any indication of having evaluated personal qualifications for job opportunities in the field.

>   Example: "I don't know what I'm interested in being ... I could stick with the science and go into research, I suppose, but I hear sales is pretty good ... something in business ... that's what I want—business."

LEVEL DESIRED (III): Any response or question which indicates that the client exhibits breadth of interest without being able to specify any choice.

>   Example: "I'm not sure what I want ... office worker, editorial assistant, proofreader, secretary ... editor."

JOB REQUIREMENTS (IV): Any response or question which indicates that the client is unaware of how to meet the requirements of certification, degrees, or experience necessary for a job in his or her field of interest.

>   Example: "I didn't realize I had to have certification to teach."

GEOGRAPHIC LOCATION (V): Any response or question which indicates that the client is unable to specify a definite geographic area where he or she would consider employment but states his or her geographic preference in such broad and vague terms as not be to meaningful.

>   Example: "I don't know ... anywhere."

JOB APPLICATION (VI): Any response or question which indicates lack of knowledge about writing a letter of application or about procedures in applying for a job.

>   Example: "Letter? You mean for a job? How do I write it?"

JOB CAMPAIGN (VII): Any response or question which indicates that the client has a lack of knowledge about planning a personal job campaign in his or her field of interest.

Example: "What do you mean by job campaign?"

SALARY (VIII): Any response or question in which the client indicates he or she has not decided what salary range he or she will accept, or in which he or she unrealistically demands a salary above the market for his or her training and experience.

Examples: "I don't know, $350, $365, $390, $410?"
"I've got a college degree now. I won't work for a publishing house unless it's $500 a week."

REGISTRATION FORMS (IX): Any response or question in which the client does not know what part of his or her background to emphasize for his or her job objective, or he or she does not see the advantage in changing what he or she has recorded when it is suggested that another phrasing would be more appropriate for his or her goal.

Examples: "What information do I put here?"
"I'd rather not change what I've already written."

REFERENCE FORMS (X): Any response or question which indicates that the client does not know to whom he or she should distribute reference forms.

Example: "I do not know whom to give it to."

(1)

PASSIVITY: Any response or question which indicates the client is placing the burden of decision, or of action, on someone else, or where he or she seems incapable of formulating a choice or is unable to initiate action for meeting job requirements and seeking job opportunities.

JOB DESIRED (I): Any response or question in which the client expresses job choice in broad and vague terms and in which he or she attempts to place the burden of decision on someone else.

Examples: "Anything . . . get me a job and I'll take it."
"Tell me what job to take and I'll take it."

FIELD DESIRED (II): Any response or question in which the client is thinking broadly or vaguely of fields and attempts to place the burden of decision on someone else for evaluating his or her qualifications for opportunities in these fields.

Examples: "Tell me what I'm qualified for."
"I'm not sure what I want to do . . . something interesting . . . something with people. . . . What should I do?"

LEVEL DESIRED (III): Any response or question in which the client is unable to make a specific choice and attempts to place the burden of decision on someone else.

Example: "You know the opportunities in English; what kind of job should I apply for?"

JOB REQUIREMENTS (IV): Any response or question which indicates that the client is unaware of how to meet the requirements of the job and field of interest and/or is unsure of the necessity for fulfilling these requirements.

Examples: "You mean to be a school psychologist, I'd have to take courses that would certify me for the city? Gee, I thought I'd qualify with my psych major."

"I don't see why I can't get a job without graduate training in counseling psychology. I know I'd be a better therapist with children than lots of psychiatrists in the field. That's ridiculous. I can do a much better job."

GEOGRAPHIC LOCATION (V): Any response or question which indicates the client is unable to specify a geographic location where he or she would consider employment and in which he or she attempts to place the burden of decision on someone else.

Example: "Professor X says I should take a job near home."

JOB APPLICATION (VI): Any response or question in which the client indicates lack of knowledge about making application for a job and where he or she attempts to put the burden of decision on someone else.

Example: "Would you make the appointment for me?"

JOB CAMPAIGN (VII): Any response or question which indicates the client never considered a job campaign.

Example: "No. What's a job campaign?"

SALARY (VIII): Any response or question which indicates the client has not decided what salary to consider and where he or she attempts to place the burden of decision on someone else.

Examples: "I don't know what salary I want. What should I ask for?"

"Professor X says I should ask for $350 a week."

REGISTRATION FORMS (IX): Any response or question which indicates the client is unable to organize his or her background for recording on registration forms in support of his or her job-seeking efforts, or indicates that he or she would prefer not to fill out the forms at all.

Example: "You say my duties on my part-time job could be important in getting a job? I was only a clerk. I don't know what to say about it."

REFERENCE FORMS (X): Any response or question which indicates that the client expects the placement office to distribute the references, or indicates that he or she would rather not ask for the references covering experiences.

Examples: "I'd rather not get any references; it would bother them."
"Will you send the references out for me?"

BIBLIOGRAPHY

Aiken, James; and Johnson, Joseph A.: Promoting career information seeking behaviors in college students. *Journal of Vocational Behavior, 3:*81–87, 1973.

Alper, Thelma G.: The relationship between role orientation and achievement motivation in college women. *Journal of Personality, 41:*9–31, 1973.

Argote, Linda M., Fisher, Joan E., McDonald, Peter J., and O'Neal, Edgar C.: Competitiveness in males and in females: situational determinants of fear of success behavior. *Sex Roles, 2:*295–303, 1976.

Ashby, Jefferson D., Wall, Harvey W., and Osipow, Samuel H.: Vocational certainty and indecision in college freshmen. *Personnel and Guidance Journal, 44:*1037–1041, 1966.

Babcock, Robert J., and Kaufman, Marilyn Ann: Effectiveness of a career course. *Vocational Guidance Quarterly, 24:*261–266, 1976.

Barker, Sandra B.: An evaluation of the effectiveness of a college career guidance course. *Journal of College Student Personnel, 22:*354–358, 1981.

Beilin, Harry: The application of general developmental principles to the vocational area. *Journal of Counseling Psychology, 2:*53–57, 1955.

Berger-Gross, Victoria; Kahn, Matthew W.; and Weare, Constance Regan: The role of anxiety in the career decision making of liberal arts students. *Journal of Vocational Behavior, 22:*312–323, 1983.

Berne, Eric: *What Do You Say After You Say Hello?: The Psychology of Human Destiny.* New York, Grove Press, 1972.

Birney, Robert C.; Burdick, Harvey; and Teevan, Richard C.: *Fear of Failure.* New York, Van Nostrand-Reinhold, 1969.

Bordin, Edward S.: The ambivalent quest for independence. *Journal of Counseling Psychology, 12:*339–345, 1965. Used with permission of author.

Bordin, Edward S.; Nachmann, Barbara; and Segal, Stanley J.: An articulated framework for vocational development. *Journal of Counseling Psychology, 10:*107–116, 1963.

Brandel, Irvin W.: Puzzling your career: a self-responsibility, self-acceptance approach to career planning. *Personnel and Guidance Journal, 61:*225–228, 1982.

Brown, Marilyn; Jennings, Jim; and Vanik, Vickie: The motive to avoid success: a further examination. *Journal of Research in Personality, 8:*172–176, 1974.

Butcher, Elizabeth: Changing by choice: a process model for group career counseling. *Vocational Guidance Quarterly, 30:*203–209, 1982. Copyright AACD. Reprinted with permission.

Cellini, James Vincent III: Locus of control as an organizing construct for vocational indecision and vocational differentiation. (Unpublished dissertation, Ohio State University, 1978.) *Dissertation Abstracts International, 39/08B,* p. 4004, 1979.

Cochran, Donald F.; Hetherington, Cheryl; and Strand, Kenneth H.: Career choice: caviar or caveat? *Journal of College Student Personnel, 21:*402–406, 1980.

Cooper, Stewart E., Fuqua, Dale R., and Hartman, Bruce W.: The relationship of trait indecisiveness to vocational uncertainty, career indecision, and interpersonal characteristics. *Journal of College Student Personnel, 25:*353–356, 1984.

Depner, Charlene E., and O'Leary, Virginia E.: Understanding female careerism: fear of success and new directions. *Sex Roles, 2:*259–268, 1976.

Donald, Kathleen, M., and Carlisle, Jane M.: The "diverse decision makers": helping students with career decisions. *Vocational Guidance Quarterly, 31:*270–275, 1983.

Erikson, Erik H.: *Childhood and Society.* New York, W. W. Norton, 1950. Used with permission.

Esposito, Ralph P.: The relationship between the motive to avoid success and vocational choice. *Journal of Vocational Behavior, 10:*347–357, 1977. Used with permission of the *Journal of Vocational Behavior* and the author.

Feather, N.T., and Raphelson, Alfred C.: Fear of success in Australian and American groups: motive or sex role stereotype? *Journal of Personality, 42:*190–201, 1974.

Feather, N.T., and Simon, J.G.: Fear of success and causal attribution for outcome. *Journal of Personality, 41:*525–542, 1973. Copyright 1973 by Duke University Press. Used with permission.

Fleming, Jacqueline: Fear of success, achievement-related motives and behavior in black college women. *Journal of Personality, 46:*694–716, 1978. Copyright 1978 by Duke University Press. Used with permission.

Forer, Bertram R.: Framework for the use of clinical techniques in vocational counseling. *Personnel and Guidance Journal, 43:*868–872, 1965. Copyright 1965 by AACD. Reprinted with permission.

Galassi, Merna Dee; and Galassi, John P.: Modifying assertive and aggressive behavior through assertion training. *Journal of College Student Personnel, 19:*453–456, 1978.

Galinsky, M. David, and Fast, Irene: Vocational choice as a focus of the identity search. *Journal of Counseling Psychology, 13:*89–92, 1966.

Gillingham, William H., and Lounsbury, Jerald E.: A description and evaluation of a career exploration course. *Journal of College Student Personnel, 20:*525–529, 1979.

Ginzberg, Eli; Ginsburg, Sol W.; Axelrad, Sidney; and Herma, John L.: *Occupational Choice: An Approach to a General Theory.* New York, Columbia University Press, 1951. Reprinted with permission.

Gottfredson, Linda S.: Circumscription and compromise: a developmental theory of occupational aspirations. *Journal of Counseling Psychology Monograph, 28:*545–579, 1981. Used with permission of author.

Gottfredson, Linda S.: *Using an Occupational Aptitude Patterns (OAP) Map to Promote Reality-Based Exploration.* (Unpublished research study, Baltimore, Center for Social Organization of Schools, The Johns Hopkins University, February 1984 draft.) Used with permission of author.

Harren, Vincent A.: A model of career decision making for college students. *Journal of Vocational Behavior, 14:*119–133, 1979.

Hartman, Bruce W., and Fuqua, Dale R.: Career indecision from a multidimensional perspective: a reply to Grites. *The School Counselor, 30:*340–345, 1983.

Hartman, Bruce W., Fuqua, Dale R., and Hartman, Paul T.: The predictive potential of the Career Decision Scale in identifying chronic career indecision. *Vocational Guidance Quarterly, 32:*103–108, 1983.

Hawkins, John G., Bradley, Richard W., and White, Gordon W.: Anxiety and the process of deciding about a major and vocation. *Journal of Counseling Psychology, 24:*398–403, 1977.

Hazel, Eva R.: Group counseling for occupational choice. *Personnel and Guidance Journal, 54:*437–438, 1976.

Healy, Charles C.: Evaluation of a replicable group career counseling procedure. *Vocational Guidance Quarterly, 23:*34–40, 1974.

Heppner, P. Paul, and Krause, Janet B.: A career seminar course. *Journal of College Student Personnel*, 20:300–305, 1979.

Hoffman, Lois Wladis: Fear of success in males and females: 1965 and 1971. *Journal of Consulting and Clinical Psychology*, 42:353–358, 1974.

Holland, John L.: A theory of vocational choice. *Journal of Counseling Psychology*, 6:35–44, 1959. Used with permission of author.

Holland, John L.: *The Psychology of Vocational Types: A Theory of Personality Types and Environmental Models.* New York, Ginn, 1966. Used with permission of author.

Holland, John L.: *Professional Manual for the Self-Directed Search.* Palo Alto, Consulting Psychologists, 1979.

Holland, John L.: *Making Vocational Choices: A Theory of Vocational Personalities and Work Environments.* Second edition. Englewood Cliffs, Prentice-Hall, Copyright 1985 pp. 2,3,4,5,29,30,136. Used with permission.

Holland, John L., Gottfredson, Gary D., and Nafziger, Dean H.: Testing the validity of some theoretical signs of vocational decision-making ability. *Journal of Counseling Psychology*, 22:411–422, 1975.

Holland, John L., and Holland, Joan E.: Vocational indecision: more evidence and speculation. *Journal of Counseling Psychology*, 24:404–414, 1977. Used with permission of senior author.

Hoppock, Robert: *Occupational Information: Where To Get It and How to Use It in Career Education, Career Counseling, and Career Development.* Fourth edition. New York, McGraw-Hill, 1976.

Horner, Matina S.: Toward an understanding of achievement-related conflicts in women. *Journal of Social Issues*, 28:157–175, 1972. Used with permission of the Society for the Psychological Study of Social Issues and the author.

Jackaway, Rita; and Teevan, Richard: Fear of failure and fear of success: two dimensions of the same motive. *Sex Roles*, 2:283–293, 1976.

Jepson, David A.; Dustin, Richard; and Miars, Russell: The effects of problem-solving training on adolescents' career exploration and career decision making. *Personnel and Guidance Journal*, 61:149–153, 1982.

Johnson, Norbert; Johnson, Jerome; and Yates, Coy: A 6-month follow-up study on the effects of the vocational exploration group on career maturity. *Journal of Counseling Psychology*, 28:70–71, 1981.

Kazin, Robert Ira: The relationship between types of indecision and interest test patterns. (Unpublished dissertation, Ohio State University, 1977.) *Dissertation Abstracts International*, 38/05B, pp. 2342–2343, 1977.

Kelso, Geoffrey I.: The influences of stage of leaving school on vocational maturity and reality of vocational choice. *Journal of Vocational Behavior*, 7:29–39, 1975.

Kimes, Harold G., and Troth, William A.: Relationship of trait anxiety to career decisiveness. *Journal of Counseling Psychology*, 21:277–280, 1974.

Kripke, Carol Fink: The motive to avoid success and its impact on vocational choices of senior college women. (Unpublished dissertation, Boston University, School of Education, 1980.) *Dissertations Abstracts International*, 41/05A, pp. 2016–2017, 1980.

Krumboltz, John D., Becker-Haven, Jane F., and Burnett, Kent F.: Counseling psychology. *Annual Review of Psychology*, 30:555–602, 1979.

Krumboltz, John D., and Schroeder, Wade W.: Promoting career planning through reinforcement. *Personnel and Guidance Journal*, 44:19–25, 1965. Copyright 1965 by AACD. Reprinted with permission.

Krumboltz, John D., and Thoresen, Carl E.: The effect of behavioral counseling in group and individual settings on information-seeking behavior. *Journal of Counseling Psychology,* *11*:324–333, 1964.

Kubis, J.F., and Hunter, G.P.: Evaluation of the client in placement work: validity and reliability. *Personnel and Guidance Journal, 34*:94–98, 1955.

LaFitte, Pat Chew; and Phillips, Bill: Assertive job-hunting: a lesson in integration. *Journal of College Student Personnel, 21*:92–93, 1980.

Levine, Adeline; and Crumrine, Janice: Women and fear of success: a problem in replication. *American Journal of Sociology, 80*:964–974, 1975.

Lipsman, Claire K.: Maslow's theory of needs in relation to vocational choice by students from lower socio-economic levels. *Vocational Guidance Quarterly, 15*:283–288, 1967. Copyright 1967 by AACD. Reprinted with permission.

LoCascio, Ralph: Delayed and impaired vocational development: a neglected aspect of vocational development theory. *Personnel and Guidance Journal, 42*:885–887, 1964. Copyright 1964 by AACD. Reprinted with permission.

Lopez, Frederick G.: A paradoxical approach to vocational indecision. *Personnel and Guidance Journal, 61*:410–412, 1983. Copyright 1983 by AACD. Reprinted with permission.

Lunneborg, Patricia W.: Career counseling techniques. In Walsh, W. Bruce, and Osipow, Samuel H. (Eds.): *Handbook of Vocational Psychology.* Hillsdale, Lawrence Erlbaum Associates, 1983. Vol. 2, *Applications,* pp. 41–76.

Macdonald, Nancy E., and Hyde, Janet Shibley: Fear of success, need achievements and fear of failure: a factor analytic study. *Sex Roles, 6*:695–711, 1980.

Mahone, Charles H.: Fear of failure and unrealistic vocational aspiration. *Journal of Abnormal and Social Psychology, 60*:253–261, 1960.

McClosky, Herbert; and Schaar, John H.: Psychological dimensions of anomy. *American Sociological Review, 30*:14–40, 1965.

McWhirter, J. Jeffries; Nichols, Eric; and Banks, N. Mark: Career awareness and self-exploration (CASE) groups: a self-assessment model for career decision making. *Personnel and Guidance Journal, 62*:580–582, 1984.

Mendonca, James D., and Siess, Thomas F.: Counseling for indecisiveness: problem-solving and anxiety-management training. *Journal of Counseling Psychology, 23*:339–347, 1976.

Menninger, William C., M.D.: Introduction: the meaning of work in Western society. In Borow, Henry (Ed.): *Man in a World at Work.* Boston, Houghton Mifflin, pp. xiii–xvi. Copyright 1964 by National Vocational Guidance Association. Used with permission of Houghton Mifflin.

Monahan, Lynn; Kuhn, Deanna; and Shaver, Phillip: Intrapsychic versus cultural explanations of the "fear of success" motive. *Journal of Personality and Social Psychology, 29*:60–64, 1974.

Morgan, Sherry Ward; and Mausner, Bernard: Behavioral and fantasied indications of avoidance of success in men and women. *Journal of Personality, 41*:457–470, 1973.

Munley, Patrick H.: Erikson's theory of psychosocial development and career development. *Journal of Vocational Behavior, 10*:261–269, 1977.

Neff, Walter S.: *Work and Human Behavior.* Second Edition. New York, Aldine Publishing Company, 1977. Used with permission.

Osipow, Samuel H.: *Theories of Career Development.* Second edition. Englewood Cliffs, Prentice-Hall, 1973, p. 293. Used with permission.

Parsons, Frank: *Choosing a Vocation.* Boston, Houghton Mifflin, 1909.

Passons, William R.: Gestalt therapy interventions for group counseling. *Personnel and Guidance Journal, 51*:183–189, 1972.

Peplau, Letitia Anne: Impact of fear of success and sex-role attitudes on women's competitive achievement. *Journal of Personality and Social Psychology, 34:*561–568, 1976.

Perovich, George M., and Mierzwa, John A.: Group facilitation of vocational maturity and self-esteem in college students. *Journal of College Student Personnel, 21:*206–211, 1980.

Pickering, Ames W., Vacc, Nicholas A., and Osborne, W. Larry: Career counseling and reality therapy: a conceptual flowchart. *Journal of Employment Counseling, 20:*154–162, 1983.

Roe, Anne: *The Psychology of Occupations.* New York, John Wiley & Sons, 1956.

Rogers, Carl R.: *Client-Centered Therapy: Its Current Practice, Implications and Theory.* Boston, Houghton Mifflin, 1979, pp. 484–487. Reprinted with permission.

Rosenberg, Howard: Games the vocationally undecided play. *Personnel and Guidance Journal,* *56:*229–234, 1977. Copyright 1977 by AACD. Reprinted with permission.

Rubinton, Natalie: Instruction in career decision making and decision-making styles. *Journal of Counseling Psychology, 27:*581–588, 1980. Used with permission of author.

Sadd, Susan; Lenauer, Michael; Shaver, Phillip; and Dunivant, Noel: Objective measurement of fear of success and fear of failure: a factor analytic approach. *Journal of Counseling and Clinical Psychology, 46:*405–416, 1978.

Salomone, Paul R.: Difficult cases in career counseling: II—the indecisive client. *Personnel and Guidance Journal, 60:*496–499, 1982. Copyright 1982 by AACD. Reprinted with permission.

Saltoun, Jane: Fear of failure in career development. *Vocational Guidance Quarterly, 29:*35–41, 1980. Copyright 1980 by AACD. Reprinted with permission.

Samaniego, Sandra: The motive to avoid academic and vocational success in Hispanic American women. (Unpublished dissertation, City University of New York, 1980.) *Dissertation Abstracts International, 41/08B,* p. 3197, 1981.

Scheier, Ivan H., and Cattell, Raymond B.: *Handbook for the Neuroticism Scale Questionnaire: The "NSQ."* First handbook edition. Champaign, Institute for Personality and Ability Testing, 1961.

Schneider, L. Ronald, and Stevens, Nancy D.: Personality characteristics associated with job-seeking behavior patterns. *Vocational Guidance Quarterly, 19:*194–200, 1971. Copyright 1971 by AACD. Reprinted with permission.

Schnitzer, Phoebe Kazdin: The motive to avoid success: exploring the nature of fear. *Psychology of Women Quarterly, 1:*273–282, 1977.

Shaver, Phillip: Questions concerning fear of success and its conceptual relatives. *Sex Roles,* 2:305–320, 1976. Used with permission of *Sex Roles* and the author.

Sherman, Pamela; Tobias, Sigmund; and Zibrin, Maria: *Fear of Success and Achievement Anxiety in Reentry Versus Non-Reentry Women.* (Research study, Center for Advanced Study in Education, City University of New York, 1982.)

Shertzer, Bruce: *Career Planning: Freedom to Choose.* Boston, Houghton Mifflin, 1977, p. 175. Used with permission.

Smith, Georgia: The effectiveness of a career guidance class: an organizational comparison. *Journal of College Student Personnel, 22:*120–124, 1981.

Smith, Robert L., and Southern, Stephen: Multimodal career counseling: an application of the "BASIC ID." *Vocational Guidance Quarterly, 29:*57–64, 1980. Copyright 1980 by AACD. Reprinted with permission.

Stevens, Nancy D.: *The Relationship of Placement Readiness to Placement Success.* (Unpublished dissertation, New York University, 1960.)

Stevens, Nancy D.: A concept of placement readiness. *Vocational Guidance Quarterly, 10:*143–148, 1962. Copyright 1962 by AACD. Reprinted with permission.

Stevens, Nancy D.: *The Relationship of Placement Readiness to Placement Success of Liberal Arts*

College Students. (Unpublished research study, Hunter College, City University of New York, 1965.)

Stevens, Nancy D.: Counseling for placement readiness. *Journal of College Student Personnel,* 7:27–32, 1966. Copyright 1966 by AACD. Reprinted with permission.

Stevens, Nancy D.: The effect of job-seeking behavior. *Journal of College Placement,* 32(4):46–50, 1972. Used with permission.

Stevens, Nancy D.: Job-seeking behavior: a segment of vocational development. *Journal of Vocational Behavior,* 3:209–219, 1973. Used with permission.

Stevens, Nancy D.: Conflict in job-seeking behavior. *Journal of College Placement,* 37(4):28–32, 1977. Used with permission.

Stevens, Nancy D., and Schneider, L. Ronald: Dynamics of job-seeking behavior. *Journal of Employment Counseling,* 4:56–62, 1967a. Copyright 1967 by AACD. Reprinted with permission.

Stevens, Nancy Duncan; and Schneider, L. Ronald: Dynamics of job-seeking behavior: moderate placement readiness. *Journal of Employment Counseling,* 4:79–85, 1967b. Copyright 1967 by AACD. Reprinted with permission.

Stumpf, Steven A., Austin, Elizabeth J., and Hartman, Karen: The impact of career exploration and interview readiness on interview performance and outcome. *Journal of Vocational Behavior,* 24:221–235, 1984.

Super, Donald E.: Vocational adjustment: implementing a self-concept. *Occupations,* 30:88–92, 1951. Copyright 1951 by AACD. Reprinted with permission.

Super, Donald E.: Toward making self-concept theory operational. In Super, Donald E.; Starishevsky, Reuben; Matlin, Norman; and Jordaan, Jean Pierre: *Career Development: Self-Concept Theory.* New York, College Entrance Examination Board, 1963, pp. 18–32.

Super, Donald E.: Vocational development theory: persons, positions, and processes. In Whiteley, John M., and Resnikoff, Arthur (Eds.): *Perspectives on Vocational Development.* Washington, D.C.: American Personnel and Guidance Association, 1972, pp. 13–33. Copyright 1972 by AACD. Reprinted with permission.

Super, Donald E., Crites, John O., Hummel, Raymond C., Moser, Helen P., Overstreet, Phoebe L., and Warnath, Charles F.: *Vocational Development: A Framework for Research.* New York, Teachers College Press. Copyright 1957 by Teachers College, Columbia University. All rights reserved, pp. 40–41. Reprinted with permission.

Tiedeman, David V.: Decisions and vocational development: a paradigm and its implications. *Personnel and Guidance Journal,* 40:15–21, 1961. Copyright 1961 by AACD. Reprinted with permission.

Travers, Robert M.W.: Perceptual phenomenological approaches to learning. In *Essentials of Learning: An Overview for Students of Education.* New York, Macmillan, 1963, pp. 451–459.

Tyler, Leona Elizabeth: *The Work of the Counselor.* Third edition. New York, Appleton-Century-Crofts, 1969.

Van Matre, Gene; and Cooper, Stewart: Concurrent evaluation of career indecision and indecisiveness. *Personnel and Guidance Journal,* 62:637–639, 1984. Copyright 1984 by AACD. Reprinted with permission.

Varvil-Weld, Douglas C., and Fretz, Bruce R.: Expectancies and the outcome of a career development intervention. *Journal of Counseling Psychology,* 30:290–293, 1983.

Walsh, W. Bruce, and Lewis, Roger C.: Consistent, inconsistent and undecided career preferences and personality. *Journal of Vocational Behavior,* 2:309–316, 1972.

Westbrook, Franklin D.: A comparison of three methods of group vocational counseling. *Journal of Counseling Psychology,* 21:502–506, 1974.

Zytowski, Donald G.: Avoidance behavior in vocational motivation. *Personnel and Guidance Journal,* 43:746–750, 1965. Copyright 1965 by AACD. Reprinted with permission.

AUTHOR INDEX

SUBJECT INDEX

187